KE
FOLK
TALES

KENT
FOLK
TALES

TONY COOPER

The
History
Press

All illustrations by Jan Cooper, to whom I dedicate this work

First published 2011

The History Press
The Mill, Brimscombe Port
Stroud, Gloucestershire, GL5 2QG
www.thehistorypress.co.uk

Reprinted 2015

British Library Cataloguing in Publication Data.
A catalogue record for this book is available from the British Library.

ISBN 978 0 7524 5933 2

Typesetting and origination by The History Press
Printed in Great Britain

CONTENTS

INTRODUCTION

I am a storyteller, not really a writer. I would usually recount these tales in front of a live audience with all the advantages that this can offer: responses from the audience; freedom to choose the appropriate story, a word or phrase to suit the mood; the odd facial expression or hand gesture; even a snatch of song or a joke inserted where suitable. The story can be compressed or extended, moulded to a specific audience.

But writing this I can't tell who you are. One of the cunning psychological tricks that all orators must learn is to look every member of the audience in the eye as you speak. Not all at once, obviously, but glancing around in a seemingly random way. The effect is that each member of the audience will be spoken to directly for a moment and be subconsciously convinced that they are the one person in the crowd who really understands and appreciates the story. This works whether the audience know of this ancient trick or not. But it won't work on you, because I can't see you, hear you or even smell you. There again, except for my photograph, you can't see me either.

Without a living listener I am reduced to the vision of a screen of words and the occasional message to the effect: 'This sentence does not appear to have a verb' or 'Have you considered rewriting this paragraph?' Damned rude I call it! No way to behave at all. I have tried gluing a paper smile to the bottom of the screen but it turns sarcastic or sardonic after a while.

As a place to collect local folk tales Kent poses some interesting problems. We have a blurred identity; we rarely boast of being Kentish; we are a mishmash of Celts, Romans, Jutes and Lowlanders and always have been. Great swathes of workers came from

Wales and the north when the coal mines opened, adding to the rich mix. Other parts of the British Isles are more distinctive. A Leeds or York local will proudly advertise themselves as a Yorkshire man or woman; the Cornish people likewise as 'Cornish'. Their traditional stories were unchanged until printing and reading became popular a couple of hundred years ago. Then they were often, as happened to the Brothers Grimm, cleaned up and sanitised for the nursery; or worse, subjected to the Disney mistreatment.

Pshaw. The best way for you to enjoy these stories is to find one you like and then someone who you like to tell it to. Don't read it aloud, that is too much like multitasking. You would be reading one sentence whilst reciting the last one and working out accent, pacing, facial expression and half a dozen other things all at the same time. You would have one eye on the text and the other on the audience; Chameleons we are not. Ok, teachers and librarians do it but is it the best they could do?

No, tell it from memory. You will automatically adjust the story for the audience in front of you; for age, background, mood and a host of other things that you don't even have to be aware of. You could make it more local or even make it more contemporary, there are no rules. For instance, 'Little Red Riding Hood' could be male, the granny maybe living in a block of flats and the wolf a precious protected species. As for the woodcutter, what an ecological disaster he could be. Don't worry about forgetting details or plot; you can always fall back on the traditional teacher's trick of saying, 'Now, what do you think happened next?' Most of the stories in here will be new to the listeners anyway; they won't spot anything but the most obvious error.

So enjoy the stories. If I am appearing live near you, do come and join in. If not, find another live storytelling performance and try that. Always remember, the words on the page are only that; they are no more real than Margitte's pipe. The true story is an experience shared by the storyteller and their audience.

Tony Cooper, 2011
www.tonycooper.net
taleweaver@homecall.co.uk

One

THE MIRROR

Many, many, moons ago there was a Celtic man walking across a stretch of marshy north-Kent land (probably near Oare). In the late afternoon, he saw a bright light shining from below a bush, as brilliant as the setting sun. It dazzled him for a moment, giving him spots before the eyes. He moved his head to look closer and the shining light faded. As his eyes adapted to the dark beneath the leaves he saw something that surprised him so much that he fell back and sat down with a thump.

There was a face looking straight back at him; a face that he well recognised. His father's face, exactly as he remembered him when his father was a young man and he was just a young boy. The image showed the freckled skin that had given both he and his father the name of Brekin; a pair of piercing blue eyes and a red moustache under a nose like a hawk's beak. How extraordinary, he thought, to find a picture of my long-dead father here. His father had died many years ago bravely defending his hamlet against raiders from the north.

He reached forward and unhooked the frame's metal chain that was wrapped around a twig. His hand felt the cold metal of the picture as he brought it closer. Yes, there was his father, so real that he could have been alive. 'Wait until my wife sees this,' he thought, 'she never did meet my father. Now she will see what a fine man he was, how bold, how noble.' He slipped the picture into the leather

bag that he wore at his waist and walked the muddy path back to his home.

Home was one of a group of rough stone huts half-sunk into the earth with low woven willow roofs covered in turf. A hole in the centre of the oval let out some of the smoke from the fire; the rest of the smoke killed off some of the pests that lived in their bedding and clothes and helped to preserve the meat and fish that hung from the roofs. As Brekin approached he could dimly see his wife at the smoky cook pot. He thought of the picture and was suddenly uncertain. It was a very unlikely find. His father had never trodden these lands; as far as he knew he had lived on the island just north of there. 'I wouldn't want to appear a fool; did I really see my father's face?' he mused. He took the picture from his pouch and made sure it was still the same. Yes, there was his Dad. He smiled and waved his fingers at the picture: 'Hello Dad,' he mouthed.

Nara was almost blinded by the smoke but she could see Brekin outside as a shape against the red evening sky. He took something from his leather bag and held it to his face. She heard him speak and saw him wave his fingers at whatever was in his hand and then put it back in his pouch. She turned back to the pot as he came into the hut. 'Hello, my dear,' he cried cheerfully.

Nara turned and looked at Brekin. Mud spattered his leggings, dirt smeared his face and he smelled of the rotten fish that he used for manure; he looked and smelled as he always did. However on this occasion Nara scolded him: 'Whoa, you stink. I can smell you even through the cooking smoke. And look at you – caked in filth. You can have some food when you have stripped and washed. Give me those clothes and out with you to the stream.'

Brekin obediently dropped his jerkin, leggings and the pouch to the floor and stomped out to the stream in fairly bad humour. While he washed Nara quickly reached into the pouch to see what Brekin had found. She could feel something hard and cold, flat like a slate. She pulled it out and looked at it. There was a heavy oval of grey metal, beaten to a dimpled flatness that showed some skilled metal-working. A finely wrought metal chain looped through a hole in one end. Nara turned it over.

The face that looked back at hers was a complete shock to her. It showed long dark hair matted with oil surrounding a pale face and deep dark eyes. A pair of full pink lips was pursed in annoyance. The woman in the picture was a beautiful sight and raised such jealous feelings in Nara that she almost threw the thing to the floor. 'He has another woman,' she thought angrily, 'right, we will see about that!' With trembling fingers she carefully and quickly put the object back into the pouch and turned back to the cooking.

Brekin lowered his head as he came back into the hut. 'All clean, where is my dinner then?' he joked.

'Get your own dinner – or perhaps your fancy girlfriend will get it for you.' Nara's voice was bitter and angry.

'What girlfriend? Who are you talking about? Has the smoke gone to your head, woman?'

'I looked in your pouch,' she sobbed, 'I saw her face in the picture. You have taken up with another woman.'

'Oh, the picture,' soothed Brekin, 'that is no woman, but a picture of my father as a young man. Same nose, same eyes, same moustache. The smoke must be in your eyes to mistake him for a woman.'

He drew the object from his pouch and looked at it. Yes, the same familiar Brekin face gazed back. 'Look, my darling, clear your eyes and see what I can see.'

He turned the frame towards Nara; she blinked and looked again. The beautiful woman was still there; deep dark eyes set in a milky skin. No man had ever looked like that. What was her Brekin thinking of? But what could she do if he denied that a woman was there? She needed help, advice from a wise woman. Outside she could hear a broken tuneless humming as an old woman ground seeds outside the neighbouring hut.

'Right,' she spat, 'wait 'til your mother hears about this!'

She snatched the picture from Brekin's hand and marched into the late evening air. There was a woman a few yards away bent double over two milling stones; it was Brekin's mother. She and Nara had argued bitterly in the past but this situation went beyond petty squabbles about how to share the food and her not producing any grandchildren yet. This was a problem – unfaithfulness – , about which all women should support each other. Men, Nara decided, are the one problem all women share. She took a deep breath and approached her mother-in-law.

'Greetings, Eoghania, mother of my husband.'

'Greetings to you, Nara, wife of my son. How goes the day for you? You look most pale, do you quicken with child?' She grinned a lascivious smile.

'Not this moon. I have more pressing problems.'

'Whatever could be more pressing than being without a child?'

'Being without a good man. Listen. Your son, my husband, has found – another woman.' Her voice spluttered into unwilling sobs; this was no way to address an elder but she could not help it.

Eoghania was enraged. 'What?! And what proofs have you of this? My boy would never do such a thing. He is a good man, always has been. Have you seen this woman? Who is she?'

'I don't know who she is. I found her picture in his pouch when he returned just now.'

'A picture, ay? A picture is not a woman. Does the picture show her as beautiful or plain?'

Nara looked at the picture and sobbed. 'She has pale skin and dark hair but her eyes are deep and lively. She is beautiful but I would kill her if she should come close to Brekin, I would scratch out those eyes.'

'Show me the picture,' Eoghania ordered.

Nara passed the frame to her mother-in-law. Eoghania turned it over in her dusty hand then held it close to her failing eyes. Back and forth she moved it until the image was clear. She scrutinised the picture then squinted with her left eye and looked again.

'Ghaaa, she's no more than an ugly old hag. Get rid of her.'

As she said it, she lifted the grinding querns and tipped the course flour into her bag. Then she put the mirror onto the bottom stone and slammed the two together again before grinding it to pieces. The sound of the stones reducing the metal and glass to powder lasted until the moon rose.

Mirrors did not become part of daily life until over 500 years later when the Romans came.

Two

KING HERLA

In the days when you could ride from Dover to Dartford without leaving the great forest there was a young King of Kent, Herla, who lived for hunting. He would ride with his men from dawn to dusk and then set-up camp to feast on their quarry. Indeed, if the animal was strong, cunning and quick he would admire its strength and skill; if the moon was full he would hunt through the whole night.

One spring there had been one wonderful chase after another, night after day. As the sun stayed up longer, so did King Herla. His older huntsmen grew tired and some returned to the castle. Eventually even Herla, young, strong and handsome as he was, was forced to rest. One cloudy afternoon, he stretched out on a mossy bank in an ancient grove and closed his eyes.

Suddenly he opened his eyes. He could hear an animal moving through the forest; he couldn't see it but he could hear it and more than that, he could smell it. Herla drew his sword and sniffed. Not a deer nor a horse, not a boar nor a badger. A goat, that's what it was. No mistaking that pungent perfume. The undergrowth parted and out trotted the most beautiful goat that King Herla had ever seen. The coat was fawn and white with a long silken beard and tresses; the eyes were slits of black in bronze; the horns and hooves were sumptuously gilded and on its back rode a tiny man.

He was no larger than a four-year-old child but he had a strong chest covered with a dappled fawn skin and a huge red beard down

to his hairy belly; at the end of his short legs were cloven feet. An intricate bronze crown sat on his copper locks. In a deep resonant voice he introduced himself.

'Hail, King Herla,' he boomed, 'you hunt well, as well as me. We are both kings, for I am Sut, the King of the Dwarves. There is earthly news that you are to be married to the daughter of the King of France when the leaves fall. I, too, shall be married soon but not until the leaves spring forth anew.'

'Hail, King Sut of the Dwarves,' said King Herla with a faint smile, 'we are both kings and are both to be wed. We have this much in common.'

'We do indeed and more. I, with my fellow dwarves, very much enjoy hunting and celebrations as much as you do. We drink and dance, we eat and play just as we have seen you do in your fine castle.'

'That must be a fine sight,' smiled Herla.

'Finer than you can possibly imagine, King Herla.' The dwarf grinned showing his diamond teeth. 'But you must see for yourself next spring. I propose that we invite each other to our weddings; yours as the days grow shorter, mine when the nights become shorter. What do you say?'

'Between two kings what could be finer? I accept your generous offer with all my heart.'

The Dwarf King drew a finely fashioned bronze horn from his cloak. 'Then let us drink deep from my cup to seal our words.'

Herla took the horn, drank half the heady brew and dizzily passed it back to the Dwarf King. The dwarf drank, gave a nod and then he and the goat suddenly disappeared.

Two seasons later King Herla and his fair French bride were in the middle of getting married. All the guests were crowded into the castle's great feasting hall when there was a heavy knock on the thick wooden door. When the door was opened, standing there was Sut, the King of the Dwarves and his vast band of dwarfish creatures. There were so many that they overfilled the castle keep and some pavilions had to be put outside in the courtyard to accommodate them. They carried gifts of exquisite golden horns and intricately carved chairs. They also brought endless amounts of roasted fowl and fine meats; the flagons of wine never seemed to empty. So much food was there that King Herla's feast was not touched. After three days of eating and dancing, stories and song King Sut gathered his tiny horde to leave. The dwarf reminded King Herla of his promise to attend his wedding as he left.

Two seasons later there was a summons from the world below. Herla and his bravest men would be the wedding guests of the Dwarf King and his tiny bride. Directions were given. They took many fine presents and rode long through wild unknown forests and twisting valleys through deepest Kent, until a great sandstone cliff blocked their way. From the cliff protruded an ancient withered yew; from a branch hung a small silver bell. No one touched the bell, yet a deep echoing chime rang through the Spring-leaved forest.

A copper-studded wooden door was suddenly there in the cliff before them. The door was swung open by unseen agencies revealing a cave. Beyond was a tunnel lit by torches leading down deep below the earth. As Herla and his men cautiously descended they heard a thousand dwarfish voices in riotous laughter and song. Down and down they went coming to a great cavern lit by a thousand lamps. A huge oak table stood in the centre where tiny men caroused in revelry. The Dwarf King welcomed them and Herla and his men joined the dancing, picking up dwarf princesses, putting them on their shoulders and whirling them around. The throng cheered.

The feasting and music lasted for three days. Wine and ale were flowing, songs were sung and jokes were told but at last it was time for King Herla and his men to leave. The Dwarf King begged Herla not to go and gave him many wonderful gifts: hawks, spears and bows and a miniature bloodhound.

'King Herla, you are like a brother to me now. I beg you to stay. The world above is dangerous to you as since your visit much has changed; on pain of death do not dismount until this bloodhound that you carry jumps down from the horse.'

King Herla hugged him close and declared that he loved him like a brother but that he was a king and that he must return to rule his land. He and his men rode up the tunnel and eventually out into the open air. They were astonished to find fields where there had once been forest and villages when they left. Their familiar lands had changed and new roads led to unknown destinations. Herla saw an old man with a flock of sheep. He stopped by him and asked, 'Old fellow, which way to the castle of King Herla?'

The shepherd stared long at the King with his mouth hanging open. Eventually in broken tongue he said, 'You speak the language of a Briton. No man has spoken as you do for many generations. Legends of King Herla say that he vanished one day and that his young wife pined away and died of a broken heart. But all this happened over 300 years ago, before the Saxons came.'

Some men cried 'Liar!' and drew their swords and dismounted but on touching the earth they crumbled to dust. It is said that King Herla and his men still ride to this day, waiting for the dwarf-ish bloodhound to jump down.

One evening, in 1983, my own wife was working late, helping with the harvest in Staple, when the earth shook with unseen passing hooves and the jingle of harness and armour. There was nothing to be seen. So perhaps, just maybe, the bloodhound still rides on the hunting horse of ancient King Herla.

Three

THE CELTIC HERO

We storytellers measure time in a different way from archaeologists, historians or scientists. We don't need to know when or where a story started. We are more interested in how often a tale has been told, so we measure in 'Grandfathers' or 'Grandmothers'. Either will do, for it is simply the time it takes for you to be old enough to sit a grandchild on your knee and tell a story that you heard on your Grandparent's knee. So a 'Grandparent' is around forty years.

Only about fifty 'Grandparents' ago, or around 2,000 years ago, there was alarm and consternation along the Kent coast. Boats were being rowed across the Channel from the land of Belgica, which would later become France. Sunlight flashed on the armour that the soldiers wore; drums beat out the rhythms of the oars. A few biremes like these had landed fifty years earlier. However, they had only beached, explored a little and returned to their boats.

This new invasion landed between the sea and the sand dunes of what is now Sandwich Bay. The boats disgorged batches of soldiers each eighty to a hundred strong. They were strong, well-trained young men who could fight like killing machines; slash, stab, slice and stamp. Yes, even their sharpened metal boots were weapons. They had fought and won all the way from Spain to Mesopotamia, they had beaten and subdued Egyptians and Huns. They were the mighty Romans.

The people who lived behind the beach were the Cantii; a tribe of Celts. They were much more likely to show extreme bravery by fighting with a feather in their hand rather than a weapon. After all; anyone can be fierce with a sharp sword or a heavy club, protected by a layer of strong metal. The Celts wore paint on their bodies and faces, not strong bronze armour and helmets. Celt-to-Celt fighting was done with bravado. 'Look,' a warrior seemed to be saying, 'I am not afraid of you. I wear nothing but a bit of fur, some paint and a fierce face. My weapon is a small feather. Think of the shame if you were to attack me with a sword. How foolish you would seem.'

This worked well amongst the Celts for hundreds of years. However, the Romans didn't seem to understand how it was supposed to work. The Celt would wave his little feather in the Romans' face in what seemed a reasonably challenging way and the rude Roman would strike him down without hesitation. Many Celts died like this.

The Romans disembarked and lined themselves up neatly on the beach; sinister, dexter, sinister, dexter. Their commander marched up and down the lines inspecting their weapons and haircuts. One young soldier, Plutus, had a strange, eager look on his face. He was staring over the commanders' shoulder.

'Look, sir, up on the sand dune. It's a man with a blue face; a Celt. Let me get him, sir?'

'Now, lad, let's not be hasty. You've just finished a dangerous sea crossing from Belgica and you still look a bit green around the gills. We will get him, all right. Flavius, come here.'

An older soldier with a face like a mouldy cabbage came forward.

'Now, Flavius, this young soldier is keen to capture that Celt up there. Go with him and try not to damage the prisoner too much. He may be useful. He may know things. Off you go.'

The two stomped up the dune clattering their swords against their armour and growling; a technique long used by the legions to terrify the enemy. The Celt disappeared as they approached. There was a silence on the sandy beach. The Roman pair also vanished over the top of the dune. The silence was broken by a short grunt and a scream. The commander smiled to himself.

A severed head rolled down the dune to the commander's feet. The commander's smile faded. He had told them to be careful, not to damage the prisoner. This head wasn't going to be talking to anyone. And why was it wearing a Roman helmet? He looked closer. Flavius! Another grunt, more screams and a second head rolled down. No helmet on this one but it was recognisable as Plutus, despite the frozen look of terror that his face showed.

The lone Celt appeared at the top of the dune. His expression could not be made out against the bright sky but the commander had the sensation that he was smiling. Right, he thought. We will see what he can do against ten trained men. He chose the most experienced, the fittest and the most vicious fighters from the hundreds on the beach and sent them up the sandy pile.

As twenty metal boots clambered up the slope, the Celt faded away over the brow. Ten sharp Roman swords and ten bronze helmets followed close behind. They disappeared from the commander's view but then a helmet flew into the air. There were screams and gurgles, hacking and slicing. There was a pause. Ten heads, some with helmets but all with surprised expressions on their dead faces, rolled down the dune.

'That Celt is tougher than he looks,' thought the commander admiringly. 'But we have numbers. Two hundred men to a boat and fifty boats make it, er, 10,000 highly trained soldiers. Surely that is more than enough for one scrawny Celt.'

He chose several rough crews, scarred and tough. One hundred armed Romans should be plenty he thought. The blue face appeared to taunt the commander from the top of the dune. On his order the hundred swarmed towards it.

Over the next fifteen minutes the air was filled with the sound of thuds, screams and gurgles. The air above the dune turned red. Through a mist of blood, body parts could be seen flying through the air. Ninety-nine heads tumbled down the slope, most looking alarmed and upset. But one Roman figure, grievously wounded but just alive, slid down to the commander's feet. He was just able, before he died, to mutter a last word or two.

'Sir,' he gasped, 'send no more men. It's a trap; a Celtic trick. There are', he choked on his blood, 'two of them. He has his *wife* with him.'

Four

PRINCESS RUSHYCOAT

The Phird King of Phannit was at feast with his queen and his three daughters. Only the youngest was actually his daughter, the other two had come with his new queen and were his stepdaughters. The King gazed drunkenly at the three lovely young princesses and wondered how they felt about him.

'Eldest daughter, how much do you love me?'

Not much, as it happened, she thought him a drunken lout but her wits gave her an answer.

'Father, I love you more than, um,' she looked about hopefully and noticed the moonlight coming though the window, 'more than the whole world.'

This pleased King Phannit and he smiled and turned to the next princess.

'And middle daughter, how mush do you love me?'

Again, not much, he was always pinching her bottom, but she thought for a moment and noticing the remains of her favourite pet piglet on the table said, 'Father, I love you, er, more than life itself.'

This pleased King Phannit too and his smile grew wider. Now the King looked fondly at his youngest princess.

'Now, my precious little one, do you love me more than the world or more than life itself?

Now she was his own daughter and she really did love him but she had to think how best to say it. Her eye wandered across the laden table and at last she said, 'Father, I love you more than meat loves salt.'

'What?' cried her father, 'am I the meat or am I the salt? I am the King! I have never been so insulted in my life. Out! Out, amongst the peasants where you belong.'

He seized her by the neck and bustled her to the castle door where he threw her out into the rainy night. Her silk dress was useless against the foul weather; her lovely dancing shoes fell apart immediately. Weeping, wet and cold she stumbled away from the castle through the fields of cabbages all the way down to the Wantsum Channel. There she found rushes growing along the banks and pulled up a bunch of them. She used a vine to tie them into a bundle and pushed her head through it.

The rain still fell on her head and dripped from her nose so she made a smaller bundle into a conical hat that completely covered her head and face. It made her look like a mobile haystack. She struggled along the bank until she came to the Wantsum Ferry. A silver ring from her finger paid the ferryman well for her trip to Grove. From there she wandered from hedge to barn across the chalk hills of Kent, eating nuts and berries and drinking ditchwater.

Weak with hunger and dizzy with fear she had little idea of where to go. Away from Phannit and her angry father was the only direction she knew. Across meadows and through dark forests, down shadowy valleys and over bright streams; for three days and nights she wandered. At last she came to a tall stone wall. In the wall was a wooden door. She knocked on the door with her slender fist. No one came. She picked up a flint and hammered it against the wood. The door flew open and there before her was a very fat woman dressed in a dirty white apron.

'What do you want? I'm busy,' screeched the cook.

A timid voice came from beneath the rush hat. 'Please, I beg you for shelter from the weather and somewhere to sleep.'

'Shelter? Somewhere to sleep? This is not the poorhouse; this is the palace kitchens of the King of Canterbury. Why should we help a haystack like you?'

'Perhaps you have work that I could do?'

'Well, nobody has washed the pans or plates since the last girl died three weeks ago. We are all much too busy. There is the pile, get to it. You can eat the leftovers if you like.'

'Thank you very much, I will do that,' said the Princess.

Afraid that word of where she was would get back to her father, the Princess kept on her rush hat and coat; the cooks all called her Rushycoat. Washing the pots and pans was horrible; the Princess was always scraping and scrubbing with her arms deep in greasy water. She slept in the huge fireplace amongst the warm cinders and ate what scraps were left on the plates. Despite all this, as the months turned into years she turned from a girl into a woman under her rushes.

One warm spring there was suddenly much to do in the kitchens. The King of Canterbury was impatient for his son, the prince, to be married to a suitable bride. Now, the Prince did all the princely things; gambled, rode and hunted, fought with sword and shield, but he never showed any interest in women at all. The King invited princesses from far and wide to Canterbury Castle for banquets and dances.

Plucked peacocks, boiled boars and fruit fancies filled the kitchens while the dirty pots and pans kept coming. The corridors above shimmered with silks and sapphires, emeralds and embroidery. The prince went to the dances and feasts and was polite to his guests but that was all; no royal female ever caught the prince's eye. Eventually, in desperation, the King threw open the invitation to all females of marriageable age.

The cooks in the royal kitchen were very much excited. Who knew who would turn the prince's head? Dresses were made, hair was curled and coloured, dancing shoes were bought and dance steps rehearsed. 'What about you, Rushycoat, are you coming to the dance?' But the Princess of Phannit was still afraid of her father. The rushes stayed on and she refused the chance of the dance.

The first feast and dance for the common women was going well, although the prince showed no interest in any partners. But then there appeared a vision of loveliness gliding into the hall.

Glossy dark hair flowed down her back; emerald earrings sparkled against her shoulders where her green, silk dress showed intricate brocade and pearls. Her feet were bare but they knew the dance steps better than any other and they twinkled on the stone floor as if they didn't need to touch it. Rushycoat had dared to take off her rushes; Princess Phannit was dancing.

The Prince was charmed by her, enchanted and enthralled. Her dark blue eyes held him, her lips promised pleasures to come and her limbs seemed lighter than air as they whirled to the music. Here, he thought, was the girl he could spend the rest of his life with. As midnight tolled the end of the dance he turned to the King to tell him the marvellous news and when he turned back – she had gone. Aghast he searched the hall and the castle but Princess Phannit had disappeared. Rushycoat was back in the kitchen, washing up.

The Prince of Canterbury asked everyone who the lovely dancer was but no one knew. He searched the city and the villages and scoured the countryside with his knights but to no avail; the lovely dancer could not be found. He had to wait until the next Saturday night and the next dance.

There she was, half an hour after all the others had arrived. They gambolled and flirted, whirled and spun. But the prince had a plan. He pulled the golden signet ring from his little finger and as they walked hand in hand to the balcony to look at the moonlit city he forced the ring onto her middle finger. It would not easily come off; she wouldn't be able to hide so easily with this royal trinket shining on her hand.

So when she again disappeared at midnight he wasn't too worried. She would soon be found. He commanded that everyone should look on all female fingers and that there would be a fine reward for the person who found the ring and her. Now, of course, there were some fingers that were never seen, deep in the washing up of the royal kitchens as they were. Rushycoat remained hidden. The reward was never claimed, Princess Phannit was never found.

The Prince was in love and love can be a terrible sickness. He couldn't sleep, he couldn't eat, his eyes grew dim and his face grew thin. He stayed in bed all day. The doctors gave him potions to help him sleep and sent to the kitchen for some chicken soup to build up his strength. The head cook in her white smock was too busy to do it so she gave the job to the undercook. The undercook hated making chicken soup, too greasy, so she gave the job to Rushycoat. While Rushycoat was skimming off the chicken fat she dropped the spoon into the broth. She had to put her hand into the warm slippery liquid to find the spoon and the royal ring slipped from her finger. The undercook took the soup away before Rushycoat realised that the ring had gone. The business of serving the prince was, of course, only to be done by the Head Cook.

The soup was carried by the head cook up the stone stairs and into the prince's bedroom. It was given to the doctor who urged him to eat just a little and dipped the golden spoon deep into the nourishing broth.

'Open wide,' encouraged the doctor and tipped the spoonful into the royal mouth. The Prince sloshed the soup around his teeth and a clink was heard. He spat out a hard object and was astounded to see his own ring, wet and fatty; but it was his own ring with his own royal crest engraved on it. The Prince immediately looked and felt better. 'My ring,' he cried, 'here is my own ring in this bowl. I will marry the one who made this soup.'

The doctor said he had requested the soup from the head cook. She was summoned to the royal sickroom to see the prince and accept his hand in marriage. She waddled into the room in a cloud of flour and cheap perfume and said, 'Your bride is here, my darling!'

The prince was a little shocked and speechless. Eventually he said, 'You are not the one I danced with and you are certainly not my bride. Who really made my chicken soup?' The cook burst into tears and admitted that she had given the task to the undercook, who was brought up from the kitchens.

A painfully thin woman was the undercook, with a nose like an eagle's beak. 'You did not make my chicken soup, did you,' asked the Prince.

'I did not,' wailed the undercook.'I asked Rushycoat to do it. I'm ever so sorry.' 'And what does this"Rushycoat" look like?' asked the prince. 'Like a haystack,' said the undercook. The prince immediately demanded that she be fetched to him.

The conical hat and a cloak of rushes came through the bedroom door. The prince nervously reached out and raised the hat. First the slender neck, then the delicate chin was revealed. The Prince's heart was in his mouth. What if she were not the one? But the lips were the ones that he had kissed; her nose was the sweet one he remembered. Her eyes were the deep blue that had charmed him before. She was the one. She shrugged off her rushy cloak for the last time and fell into his arms. There were kisses and hugs and plans of marriage, all the things that young lovers do.

Of course the wedding was to be magnificent, lasting for three days with fiddles and drums and wonderful food for all. But the new bride had a request for the head cook.

'Now cook,' said the new bride, 'I washed your horrible dishes and pans for years and ate only scraps the while. Now you can do a favour for me. Tonight the King of Phannit will arrive at the wedding banquet with his daughters. Cook all the food as usual but for King Phannit let all his food be unsalted.'

The cook raised her eyebrows at this but did exactly as she was asked.

The feast was going well. Game broth in bird-shaped bowls was served to all. King Phannit ate his broth and made an odd face. He turned to his neighbour at the table and asked, 'How does your soup taste? A bit bland, isn't it?'

'No, no it is the finest since my grandmother's cook passed away,' replied the knight. 'Full of flavour and spices; it is a veritable meal in a bowl.'

'May I try a spoonful, to taste whether or not it is the same as mine?' asked King Phannit.

'Of course,' said the knight.

There was nothing bland about the knight's soup. The King tasted his own soup again. It was just as tasteless as before. 'Perhaps the fish will be better,' he thought.

The fish was no better, nor the meat nor the vegetables. As he ate, the King slowly realised what was missing – the salt. His thoughts went back to when salt had been mentioned at a feast before; at his own feast with his three daughters many moons ago. He remembered what his own youngest daughter had said when he had asked her how much she loved him 'More than meat loves salt.' And now he knew that she had loved him more than any other. His heart felt as if it was going to break; he should never have thrown her out into the storm. He had heard nothing of her since; maybe she had died. Tears brimmed over and dripped down his cheeks and nose.

As he cried he felt a pair of young arms reach around his neck and shoulders from behind. Royal bracelets decorated the wrists. A face nestled next to his and other eyes cried into his food. He turned to look. It was the new bride of the Prince of Canterbury. She whispered into his ear.

'Now you know how much meat loves salt perhaps you will realise how much I loved you, my darling father. And I love you still and forgive you for all.'

Both father and daughter salted the food with their tears and all was well with them, the marriage and the county.

Five

DEATH IS STRONGEST

About 700 years ago most men in Kent were ex-soldiers. We had just finished the Hundred Years War, which had been fought by rough conscripted peasants, not the noble knights of the past; so it was very likely that you, your brothers, your father and even his father would all have been soldiers. People were tough; they had to be, those who weren't strong were dead. They were hardy folk living in harsh times. Then came the Black Death, which carried away almost a third of the Kentish population.

It was at this time that three men were sitting in a public house in Maidstone drinking ale and being generally offensive to anyone within range. They were Fisk, Lark and Rob; Fisk and Lark were brothers, whilst Rob was their cousin and all three were thieves.

They did not pick locks to steal nor use clever scams; they weren't even deft enough to lift purses. They did not burgle houses nor did they have the skills to forge fake coins. They weren't bright enough to do anything like that. No, they just waited to see what they wanted and they took it. They were well armed and strong enough to go up against just about anyone.

On this day they were arm wrestling at the table, arguing about who was the strongest. They started to push and punch each other. Their voices grew louder, drinkers were jostled, a table tipped and beer was spilt. The eldest brother, Fisk, pinned his brother's throat against the wall and shouted, 'I am the best of us and we are the best of the land. What am I?'

Lark's voice was strangled and hoarse, 'You are the ckkk … the best. Let me go.'

Fisk dropped his sibling to the floor. 'Remember that well. I am stronger than all others.' He kicked Lark in the ribs. 'And who is the strongest mob in the land?'

'We are,' groaned Lark.

A small voice came from the people surrounding them. A tiny girl had spoken: 'Death is stronger than any of you.'

Fisk spun round glaring at everyone. 'Who said that?'

'I did,' said the girl. She was about five years old and was half wrapped in her mother's skirt. One hazel eye watched Fisk.

'And you, little speck, how would you know how strong Death is?' he asked.

'Cos last month Death came and took my father and my two uncles. In just one day. Now both them uncles was enormous and strong and me dad wasn't no weakling neither. But they all died when Mr Death came by. So he must be the strongest of all.'

Fisk gave the girl a withering look: 'I've seen statues of your Mr Death in the church graveyard and he looks to be all bones. No muscles on him at all. I could beat him with one arm tied behind my back. Any of us three could; blindfolded. Where is this Death?'

'He is here in the town and abroad in the county. He is everywhere,' the girl's mother said bitterly.

'That just makes him easier to find, then. Come on lads, we could do with stretching our muscles. Let's 'ave 'im. We've a fight to come.'

The three went out into the town asking everyone if they had seen Death. Some ran away, others pretended they had gone deaf and a few said that Death had taken their family or friends but had moved on. That afternoon the three strode on into the countryside amongst unploughed fields, starving cattle and broken-down farms. As they entered a dark wood down a narrow path a voice could be heard coming closer, shouting as loud as it could. The three slipped behind trees as it came near. 'DEATH, DEATH!'

The bushes parted and out burst a wizened old man, with his sparse hair tangled and his eyes staring madly. Rags draped his scrawny body and his dirty bare feet pounded the path as he ran. Spittle flew from his toothless mouth as he screamed hoarsely, 'DEATH, DEATH!'

Rob took hold of a fallen branch and as the ancient passed by he tripped him by pushing the branch between his legs. The man crashed to the ground with an awful cry. The three quickly surrounded him. Fisk thrust his face close to the old man: 'What are you shouting about? If you've seen Death you'd better tell us where he is, 'cos we want to find him and show 'im who's the strongest.' They gave him some encouragement with their boots. The old arms wrapped around the head and the bony knees pressed against the narrow chest. The voice was muffled.

'Sirs, sirs, I am no more than a hermit. Hurt me no more, I pray you. I will tell you of Death and where he can be found, I swear.' Fisk gave him another kick for luck. 'And will you speak the truth, old man? Where is Mr Death today, do you claim?' he demnded.

'Sir, he rests in a cavern under a hill yonder. Follow the path and keep to the left all the way and the cave will appear before you. But sirs, do not go, I beg you. Disaster awaits you; you will all die. Die, I tell you. Die.'

'Listen, you worm, we have fought Frenchmen, excise men, Dutchmen and sailors. We beat four big farmers over at Ashford market then stole their cattle and their daughters. We are not afraid of a bundle of old bones, no matter what his reputation. Come on, lads,' Fisk replied

They left the old man in a heap and strode off down the path. As they walked Rob stripped the fallen branch to make himself a club, Lark sharpened his dagger and Fisk rolled his sleeves up and punched a few trees for practice. In twenty minutes they had come to the cave. A low opening in the sandstone cliff where the rock had collapsed formed the entrance; beyond all was dark and silent. Fisk leaned closer and bellowed into the cavern.

'Mister Death! Mister De-ath! Yoo-hoo. We are the Maidstone Lads, come to have a little chat with you. Come out here and

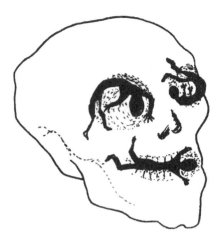

join us.' His voice echoed back from the gloom. They listened but there was no other sound but a sparrow's chirrup from a tree. 'Mister De-ath! We hear you are strong, maybe the strongest of all. Come out here and show us your big muscles.'

The other two sniggered. Lark took courage and shouted from behind Fisk, 'We've seen your picture. You're nothing but a bag of bones, you are!'

There was still no sound from the cave. Fisk beckoned to the others and bent under the shallow opening. Slowly they eased into the cave letting their eyes adapt to the dark. As soon as their bodies were no longer blocking the entrance they all let out gasps. The feeble light illuminated a glistening heap of metal; incorruptible and clean as the day it had been formed. Gold coins piled up, spilling across the dirt floor; thousands of them. Wide golden plates and delicate goblets glittered behind the heap. Lark whispered, 'No wonder the old man said to stay away and warned us of death. He wanted to keep his fortune; or rather our fortune.

The three sat down around the heap and Lark was the first to reach out and pick up a coin. He looked closely at it, weighed it in his hand then put it into his mouth and bit it. His strong teeth left no dents in the metal. 'It's gold, right enough;

a king's ransom in gold. How many coins do you reckon is here, Fisk? Must be two, maybe three thousand pieces?'

Fisks' eyes shone with greed. 'I shall buy a ship and become a pirate on the high seas. No more robbing the poor for me; I shall rob the rich.' said Fisk. 'How will you spend your share, Brother Lark?'

'A castle for me,' replied Lark, 'with high walls, a moat and a drawbridge. Guards will constantly protect my fortune from thieves like us. What of you, Cousin Rob?'

Rob was slow to answer. 'A farm; a farm and maybe a wife; a couple of cows, some pigs, a few fields of barley or oats. Some chickens, a pond with ducks and some little children to hand it all on to; and maybe a good night's sleep without my conscience being pricked.'

'Nagh, you've always been soft. What a waste. Now, how much is here? Lark, you are good at the counting; how shall it be divided?' asked Fisk.

Lark looked at the mound of treasure. 'The only sure way is to each take one coin in turns.'

'But that will take many hours,' spat Fisk, 'and we shall need food and drink. My stomach is restless at the thought of it. We cannot go to the town and leave this unguarded; who knows who else may meet the old hermit and what he may say? Thieves like us will be bound take it. Cousin Rob, take these coppers to the shops and buy us wine, bread and meat. We brothers will bravely stay to protect our fortune.'

When Rob had left for the town the brothers sat and stared at the gold. The heap seemed somehow smaller than when they had first seen it. They pulled the heavy coins into three roughly equal heaps and looked at them. Then they pushed them all into one heap and then divided that into two heaps.

Fisk looked at Lark and said 'Looks better as two heaps rather than three, don't it?'

'Yea,' said Lark. Without another word they started to sharpen their daggers.

Rob reached the town and bought roast meat, bread and a bottle of good red wine. At the apothecary shop he bought a little package of powerful poison. He pulled the wine cork out with his teeth and carefully tipped the poison in. He held the bottle up to the light and gently shook it. The powder dissolved leaving the wine clear. He put the cork back in the bottle, put it with the meat and bread into his bag and headed back towards the cave.

'Soft, eh? I'll teach you soft,' he thought.

The brothers heard him coming and hid each side of the cave entrance. Rob called, 'Lads, we have fine fare to share,' as he bent to enter the cave but no answer came. He leaned in and then the brothers stabbed together; one to the throat and the other to the heart. Rob gasped and struggled to catch his last breath before sinking to the ground.

Fisk pulled the cork from the wine bottle and poured generous amounts into two golden goblets. The toast was made: 'To the dear departed,' the goblets clinked together and they both drank deeply from the poisoned wine, to the memory of their dear, dead cousin and their fortune.

In this way Death was, and always will be, the strongest.

Six

WHAT CAN YOU SEE?

Mr. Gilbert Willet was an old Canterbury merchant. He was wealthy and married to an attractive young wife, yet somehow, he was deeply dissatisfied with his life. He had recently visited the fine house of a business rival out beyond the city walls and after a good lunch they had stood in the rival's garden on the side of Harbledown Hill. Below them could be seen the Kentish fields, the woods and the orchards, spread out for miles in the sweet, clear country air.

In contrast all you could see from Mr. Willet's garden in the city were the walls, roofs and chimneys of the surrounding houses, shops and factories. The air down there was never fresh; smoke blurred and tainted everything. You could tell which way the wind was blowing just from the smells; from the north was the yeasty odour of brewing hops; button-factory bone dust blew in from the east; leather tanning fumes came from the west and the distinctive stench of hoof and horn glue seeped from the south.

You see, Canterbury lies in a dip between two hills; St Thomas' Hill is to the west and to the east is St Martins' Hill. A tall, thick, strong wall of stone and flint, left by the Romans, surrounds the city. This is all very well for defence but it means that no one who lived in the town had a breeze or a view of the lush countryside from their houses or gardens; maybe just a glimpse of St Martin's Church with the old windmill behind it or the village of Harbledown. The walls take much of the breeze. So smoke and smells gather over the city, nestled by the hills and the city wall.

So there was not much to see from the merchant's house beside the river off Stour Street. An apple orchard filled half his garden and a few days after his visit to the rival's house he was walking there with Isabelle, his lovely young wife. A servant, Luke, carried a tray of drinks and sweetmeats behind them as they cast about for the best spot to eat; they wanted to be shaded by the tall apple trees but also be away from the acrid smell of burning feathers that floated over the wall.

'Over here, my man, put it all down here. Now, what do we have? A fine pastry or a glass of wine for you, my dear? What do you fancy?'

She couldn't tell him what she really fancied; she blushed and glanced sideways at the servant. Luke's head was bent over the tray, his shock of dark hair falling across his eyes. He swept it back with a casual flick that made her heart leap. They had accidentally touched hands passing the collecting tray in church twelve months before and something magical had flown between them. Since then there had been little more than glances and smiles but after church last Sunday they found themselves alone for a moment under a spreading yew tree and they had kissed. Oh, the sweetness of it! Kissing her husband was like kissing a pair of raw sausages and he always tasted stale; she delicately shrank from it when she could.

Luke, in contrast, had tasted of brandy and cherries and his clever tongue had tickled hers and made her shiver with pleasure. He was a Whitstable lad; not high-born but the son of a fine boat-builder and he was clever, handsome and strong. She wanted him in so many ways; to walk with, hand-in-hand, to talk and to laugh with but most of all to take him to her bed. However, there was never an opportunity for any of this. The merchant kept a close eye on his wife and as a matter of course he made sure all the servants were always kept busy. Just half an hour together was all they craved. They quivered with desire.

The breeze changed direction and the little orchard filled with the stench of tanning chemicals. Isabelle choked a little and asked for some water. The servant was sent off to fetch some from the well and the couple walked under the tallest apple tree in the garden where the air was fresher. The servant returned from the well with the water; she sipped some but said that the stink was still at the back of her throat. Isabelle put her head back and gargled. As she looked up she noticed a perfectly ripe apple at the very top of the tallest tree. An idea occurred to her.

'Dearest husband, my throat is still terribly sore from the awful chemicals. I am sure that the juice of that apple far above would sooth me. Would you, my love, climb up and fetch it for me?' Her long lashes made promises and her smile was inviting.

Mr. Willet gazed up. 'Ah, well, that is a very tall tree and the apple is at the very top. We have no ladders that long; the tree itself must be climbed. Would not that apple do?'

He pointed with his desiccated claw of a hand to a lower apple on another tree; it was smaller and nowhere near as ripe.

'The smells down here will have spoilt the flavour of that one. I must have the apple from the top of the tree.'

She choked a little to emphasise her distress. The merchant harrumphed and went off to see if his two ladders could be bound together, leaving his wife with Luke. They casually wandered through the trees coming closer as they strolled. She murmured into his ear, he smiled and nodded. They parted as the merchant returned, empty handed. The servant approached the merchant.

'I beg your pardon, sir, but this remarkable tree has branches as regular as the rigging on a boat. It would make for easy climbing. If you would give your permission I should like to pick the apple for your lady. I am not afraid of the height, sir. Many a tall mast have I climbed.'

The merchant leaned his bald head back and regarded the tree. He wondered what the view was like from the top; above the smoke and smells you should be able to see a long way. 'Yes, yes, up you go. And as you climb you can tell me what you can observe from up there. Describe the view to me. You should be able to see for miles.'

Up went the servant calling out what he could see as he climbed. He was quick and nimble and soon he called down, 'Sir, I can see into the tannery yard. A horse hide is stretched out to tan in the sun.'

'Yes, yes; higher, higher boy. What can you see?' the Merchant demanded

'Past the cathedral the Stour flowing out towards Sturry, sir, on its way to Stourmouth, Sandwich and the sea.'

'And the other way. What can you see that way?'

'The Stour again, sir, flowing past Thanington-Without, through cow fields towards the city.'

'Go up and get that apple. My wife chokes; higher, higher. What can you see?'

'The city below laid out like a map, smoke drifting upwards, carts and wagons in the streets around. I have the apple, sir.'

'Can you see anything else before you come down?'

'Well, now I look down there is something that I can see – but I cannot speak of it aloud.'

'Cannot speak of it? I am your master. I command you to tell me what you can see.' There was a pause.

'Well, sir, I can see you, sir.'

'Well, what of it? Of course you can see me, you ninny. Why can you not describe me from above?'

'It is unseemly, sir, to speak of what I can see – you doing.'

'Doing? Doing? All I am doing is standing in my own orchard looking up at a fool.'

'I beg your pardon sir but I can see you doing – other things.'

'Other things? Other things? What are you speaking of, you idiot.'

'The actions of a married man, sir.'

'What actions of a married man? You are talking nonsense, lad. Come down at once.'

'The actions that a man may perform – um – on his honeymoon.'

'Drinking? Travelling? Eating? That is what we did on our honeymoon, my man.' He had been fairly old when they were wed.

To be blunt, sir, and forgive me for these words, but I can see you making love to your wife, sir. Your clothes and hers are scattered on the ground and I can see your flesh, sir, and the bare skin of your wife. You are both – jiggling together.'

Now Mr. Henry Willet and Isabelle had not 'jiggled together' for some considerable time and he was not entirely sure that he was still capable of 'jiggling'. He decided to ask for more details.

'I can assure you that there is no jiggling going on down here. We both stand here fully clothed a few yards apart. However, this vision that you see – tell me – does my wife seem pleased with the situation?'

'Well sir, her mouth is open and smiling and she is grasping you to her body with a will. Her face is flushed, dew is on her brow, her eyes sparkle and little moans can be heard. I would say that she is very pleased with the situation, sir.'

'Yet down here she appears as calm and composed as ever, pressing a blossom to her sweet nose. How extraordinary. And how do I look? Am I pleased, do you think, with the situation?'

'Sir, you are transformed. Your back is straight, your belly is flat and your hair returned to the abundant dark brown that you must have sported in your youth. Sir, I truly believe this tree to be bewitched, to engender visions that reflect its owners desires and wishes. Oh, I wish you could see these wonders for yourself, sir, after all it is your tree.'

'Could you not help me to climb up, you are a strong lad. I could take it slowly. Yes, come down now and assist me.'

Within a few minutes Luke was on the ground. But it took almost an hour of pushing and levering, cursing and sweating, rope tying and hauling, swearing and struggling before Mr Willet was at the top of the tree. He gave the surrounding views a cursory glance or two but was soon parting the leaves to see below.

There. What Luke had said was true. There was his dear wife Isabelle with her legs and arms bare, spread out on the soft grass. On top of her was a man's figure with, yes, dark hair and plenty of it. Indeed the back was straight and the buttocks were moving with youthful energy, just as he had been able to do when he was young. What a vision! He could hear his wife's cries, 'Oh Oh Oh.' How well she was being pleased. He called out to her.

'My darling, you will scarce believe what pleasure this magical vision shows us doing. What are you really doing?'

She breathlessly called back, 'I – am – chasing – a – bright – butterfly. I – have – near – caught – it.'

'You are such a child, my dear. Luke? What are you up to?'

'Sir, I am – helping her – to catch the – fluttering thing.'

'Splendid. Chase on my beloved, chase on. What a wonderful afternoon; you with your butterfly and me with my enchanted tree. Who would wish to live outside the town now? I declare that I shall climb this magical tree every day and you shall dally in the garden below. What say you, my love?'

'Yes,' she cried, 'yes, yes, yes, yes, yes!'

Seven

GREY DOLPHIN

We have had many marvellous Lord Wardens of the Cinque Ports over the centuries; Winston Churchill, the Duke of Wellington and Elizabeth the Queen Mother all inherited their honoured positions from princes, knights and lords. One of the first was a man with a short temper and a fine horse. The short temper belonged to Sir Robert, Baron de Shurland. The fine horse's name was Grey Dolphin. The two had been to the Crusades together and fought with much bravery. Their strange story is this.

In 1337 a drowned, sea-stained body was washed up by the tide on the bank of the River Medway at Chatham. It often happened; sailors and fishermen never learned to swim, preferring to die quickly if lost at sea. They lead dangerous lives and besides which the Medway was a common resting place for the victims of mortal crimes. Like most of the corpses found he had no recognisable face; the shrimps, crabs and lobsters had dined well. The tattered remains of his clothing suggested that he had once been a seaman. He was interred near the shrine of St Bridget by Father Fothergill who was assisted in the task by the town clerk, Emmanuel Saddleton.

That night Emmanuel Saddleton was getting ready for bed at around midnight when a vision of St Bridget herself appeared glowing by his bed. The apparition was holding a bunch of white flowers but looked and sounded very annoyed and she ordered him

to dig up the corpse that they had buried that day and cast it back into the river.

'Your man,' she said, 'has died in mortal sin and should never be rested near me own holy body.'

'But are you not the patron saint of boatmen?' protested Emmanuel.

'To be sure, but only of the ones who pray hard.' said the stern Irish saint. 'Do you not know that I'm also the patron of babies, poets, blacksmiths, cattle, scholars, midwives, chicken farmers, children whose mothers are mistreated by their fathers, mariners, dairymaids, fugitives, infants,' she took a deep breath, 'Leinster, milk maids, nuns, all of the many poor, sailors, travellers, watermen and the whole of Ireland. Do you not think that is enough for one small saint? Now get that sinful body and throw it back into the river.' Having said her piece she disappeared.

Amazed and alarmed Emmanuel told Father Fothergill the next morning and together they obeyed her wishes on the next flowing high tide.

For three days the corpse drifted up and down with the tides between Sheerness and Gillingham Reach until it beached near Eastchurch, along the coast from Minster on the Isle of Sheppey. Now this land was owned by Sir Robert, Baron de Shurland and Lord Warden of the Cinque Ports. He sent his servant, Periwinkle, to have a grave dug 20ft deep, to throw the stinking body in and to send for Father Fothergill to perform the burial service. When the friar arrived Sir Robert ordered him to say his prayers and bless the body. Father Fothergill did not want to disobey a baron but he recognised the corpse and there were St Bridget's wishes to consider too.

'My Lord, I recognise this soul. I buried him in Chatham a few days ago but St Bridget appeared in a vision to the town clerk and commanded that he be cast back into the river. So we did. I am a holy man; I must obey the saints, sir. I will not say a service for this soul.'

Sir Robert was not used to being refused. His face turned red. His eyes bulged. He tried to draw Tickletoby, his famous two-handed sword, from its sheath to slay the disobedient priest but it would not come free. Perhaps St Bridget was exerting an influence. Sir Robert, furious, dismounted and booted the priest so hard in the backside that he fell into the open grave and broke his neck. The Baron, still in a fury, had the grave filled in and went back to his house for his supper.

Saint Bridget was perhaps annoyed that the life of the priest had been lost despite her staying the Baron's arm; perhaps there is gossip amongst saints. Whatever the reason, the vision of St Augustine appeared that night to Abbot Adselm in his Canterbury bed and demanded to know why one of his priests was buried in the same grave as an unshriven corpse. Abbot Adselm had no idea what the saint was talking about so Augustine explained about Sir Robert de Shurland, Father Fothergill and the corpse and demanded that he inform Pope Boniface VII, the sheriff, and the coroner and have something jolly well done about it.

So Abbot Adselm went to the Sheriff with this strange tale and explained what the Saint had said should be done. The Sheriff was a bold, brave man but he knew that the Baron could be hot-headed and brutal, so he gathered a strong band of locals together to help him tackle the fierce Sir Robert. When the locals and the Sheriff arrived at his Eastgate Castle the Baron simply shut the doors, had the drawbridge raised and the portcullis dropped, and ignored all hammering at his gate and every demand. He had been to the Crusades; he had been through sieges before. He carried on with his lunch as if nothing was happening then he went to bed for a snooze.

The besiegers were still there when he awoke in the late afternoon so he unsheathed Tickletoby and with a few retainers routed the Sheriff and his men before retiring for a substantial supper.

Sir Robert knew that even if the Pope demanded action against him that the King, Edward Longshanks, needed him for the war against France. Besides, King Edward had been insulted by Pope Boniface and wouldn't care if he was excommunicated. All Sir Robert needed was a pardon from the King and all would be well. But the King was out at sea.

Longshanks was at that moment sailing down the Thames to inspect his massed army encamped along the North Kent shore ready to attack France. His royal barge was anchored about 2 miles offshore from Eastgate. All the local boats had been taken by the camping soldiers to be broken up for firewood; so Sir Robert mounted Grey Dolphin and rode him straight into the sea. The bold horse plunged through the waves as if he were a dolphin, eventually reached the King's craft and swam round it three times while Sir Robert shouted his request for a pardon to the King.

Edward Longshanks was impressed by the bravery of both the Baron and the horse. He agreed to square the situation with the Archbishop of Canterbury and write a royal pardon if Sir Robert would agree to come and help him fight the French and later the Scots. Sir Robert readily agreed and swam Grey Dolphin back to the shore in triumph.

As he rode the horse onto the beach there was a strange figure standing on the sands waiting for him. It was an ancient wise woman draped in a filthy shawl; her nose was hooked, her hair matted and flies buzzed around her stooped body. But her piercing grey eyes held his as she cackled a dire warning that froze Sir Robert's hard heart: 'Grey Dolphin must have been possessed of the Devil to swim you that far. He has saved the life of you but he will also, heh heh heh, be the death of you, Baron. Beware!'

Sir Robert snorted in derision but the words echoed in his head as he rode along the beach. The hag was surely mad, but how had she known of his success with the King? Maybe she was right, that Grey Dolphin would kill him. Could his fate be avoided? Yes, there was something he could easily do about that! He dismounted, drew his sword, Tickletoby, and in one clean blow beheaded his horse. Now let's see the old hag's prophesy come true, he thought. Leaving the carcase and head to wash in the tides he returned to Eastgate and prepared to go to war.

A year later the war in France was over but there was still fighting to be done against William Wallace in Scotland. It was two weary years before the Baron disembarked at Sheppey and when he did he was pleased to see the old hag once again waiting on the beach. He could now crow to the silly old woman that her prophesy had not, and could not ever, come true. She was sitting on a rock and as he approached he took a deep breath – and she vanished.

Thwarted, the Baron gave the stone a mighty kick. His boots had been worn thin by his years at war and something pierced the leather and stabbed him in the toe. As he looked closer he could see that what he had kicked was not a rock – it was the bleached skull of a horse. The deep cut had been caused by a sharp fragment of horse's tooth. He limped back to Eastgate where he was treated with potions and was leached but, despite having his toe amputated, gangrene set in and within a month he was dead. The prophecy had been fulfilled. There is no doubt in the minds of Sheppey people whose skull that was.

You can see the Baron's likeness in stone on the south wall of Minster Abbey. Emerging from the stone next to him is a carving of a horse's head.

Eight

GENEROUS

Stand on the white cliffs of Dover; look in the direction of the rising sun and on a clear day you will see similar cliffs shining from across the Channel. There was once land between these cliffs; you could walk the twenty-three marshy miles to France without getting your feet particularly wet. But after an earthquake and landslide washed away the chalk hills a deep and dangerous stretch of water kept the sides apart. Known in France as 'La Manche' ('The Sleeve') and on the British side as 'The Straights of Dover'; the currents were fierce, the shifting sand banks numerous and the winds strong and gusty. Many courageous sailors drowned on the sharp rocks that littered both shores.

Now, many moons ago there was a knight, an honourable fellow, who loved his lady dearly. Unusually for the times he thought of her as his equal, and he treated her as such.

'All I ask is that you do not dishonour me,' he said, 'but in all other ways your will is your own; do as you like.'

But she was also loved by a knave, who was not nearly so honourable. The lady was left worried and sad when her husband crossed the salty Sleeve to fight the foul smelly English. It wasn't the English that worried her; her husband was a trained fighter and they were only peasants. No, it was the journey that gave her concern. She knew that The Sleeve was a treacherous channel of sandbanks, wrecks, strong currents, wild winds and jellyfish

from Cap Gris-Nez to the White Cliffs of Dover.
While her friends gaily danced and played 'pass
the posset' she retired to a secluded arbour, bit
her lip and distractedly tied knots in her fennel
sandwich. Seeing her distress the knave was
soon by her side. 'Why so sad, my frootkin?'
quizzed the knave.

Her voice was no more than a sob,
'My knight braves the toothsome rocks
and nasty things in The Sleeve and you
call me your frootkin which I am not.
I'm his frootkin, you cheeky whelk.'

'But I can save your precious knight
for a favour; say a squeeze and a kiss. I
know of a wise sorcerer deep in the countryside whose conjuring would be able
keep your chap safe from the toothsome
rocks. For no more than a promise of a
favour I would go to see him for you. Would you like me to do
that? Only if you really love him, that is?'

'I do love him, I do, I do,' she whimpered.

'Then I shall go to the sorcerer forthwith. It is a very long way
and will be extremely dangerous but I will be thinking at all times
of your favours when I return, so I shall be brave.' Up pointed his
nose and away he went.

He travelled for weeks through Gallic swamps and forests and
when he stayed at an inn he was soon playing a local game of 'Rob
the Twit' and losing most of his gold.

So when he reached the sorcerer he was both poor and nervous.
A large, damp cave swathed in exotic curtains was the wizard's
home and the knave entered anxiously. There, seated on a fancy
throne, was a man with a huge nose, bushy eyebrows and a vast
smouldering hat. The knave bowed deeply, explained the problem
about the knight and the Channel, also about the lady and the
bargain; so the wizard blew through his moustaches, slipped
behind a curtain and checked the tide tables. Soon there were

clouds of magical smoke, a bright flash and a low moaning noise (a conjuring accident caused the pained groan). The sorcerer reappeared with no hat and a pair of singed eyebrows. He spoke in slow, magical tone:

'Your man will arrive safely if he sails on the morning of first day of April. That will be 200 gold pieces, please,' said the wise one, sucking his elbow. Now, our knave had only two gold pieces left and one of them was a bit dodgy.

'My magnificence, are you really, as you claim, an all-seeing wizard?' the knave asked with a sly smile.

'O yes, of course. I know the ways of the planets, the languages of the birds and much, much more.'

'So if I slide off now without paying you anything you won't worry will you? You will, with your magical powers, see me everywhere I go. And I am a gentleman, I assure you. I'll be back with the money in a trice.' Bowing deeply he slowly reversed out of the cave and then ran as fast as his legs would carry him, desperately trying to remember what a trice was.

Well, many moons later he got back to the lady and explained how dangerous and expensive it all had been but he said that her husband would be safe. When the knight was safely home he would expect her to come to him and he would claim his favour.

In spring, on a particularly high tide, her man came back safely across La Manche. In pitiful tears she met her husband on the shore.

'What's up, frootkin?' he murmured.

'I have promised my favours, my honour – my whole self to a knave,' she wailed.

'Why? Why have you promised this? Is not my burning love enough?'

'He said he could protect you; to save you from the toothsome rocks of La Manche. He said he knew of a distant sorcerer who could keep you safe. I thought – I thought my honour may save your precious life.' Her sobs wrenched at his heart.

'Then a virtuous promise given for a noble reason must be kept,' he announced through tight lips. 'Go to the knave and honour the debt but don't you dare enjoy it!'

So she went. The knave was very pleased to see her and he quivered with desire. Her voice was trembling and low: 'My husband is home safe as you promised and for this I thank you,' she said. 'Your reward is, as we agreed, me. My husband knows of this and he insists that the debt must be paid.' Her voice broke as she loosened her bodice.

The knave was shocked that the knight would approve of the promise. He considered what he really wanted; to be a gentleman, an honourable knight like her husband. He gazed at her milky flesh, thought for a moment and then said, 'I cannot show myself to be less generous than your knight. I thus absolve you of your promise.'

She kissed him on the nose and squealed all the way back to her knight and told him the good news. They celebrated with wine and food then took themselves to bed for – a nice rest I expect.

The knave went reluctantly back through swamps and forests to the cave of the sorcerer and explained that although the rocks had vanished and the knight had survived, he hadn't had a nice time and, possibly worse than that, he'd got no money at all to pay him with. He waited with eyes tight shut to be turned into something nasty.

'Your man arrived safely. Yet you received neither kiss nor favour? You are a twit. But I cannot be seen as the least generous of us all. Thus I absolve you of your debt. BEGONE!'

So there we were; the knight treated his wife as an equal, the wife tried to give her virtue to save her husband, the knave did not take the favour that he had earned and the wizard refused his payment – but who of all these was the most generous?

Nine

The Princess and the Fool

Many moons ago there was a King of Canterbury and he had a daughter, the Princess. She was nearly eighteen years old and lovely, with dark almond eyes and flowing auburn tresses. She was also very clever. The King was old, with dark hooded eyes and sparse white hair. He was a little slow of thought but also a worried man. His princess should by now, he thought, be married. If she did not have a male child before he died his entire kingdom would go to his beastly brother, the King of Phannit; unthinkable.

Oh they came, the ardent young men. There was always one or two young fellows hanging around the castle waiting to see her; dressed in their silks and furs, combing their hair and breathing into their hands to test whether their breath was sweet. But when they met her she was only interested in one thing – their minds. She could not bear the idea of living with a person without a wit – she had had enough of that with her father.

So each swain would come before her and be asked three questions and be given a task. The questions were different every time, she made them up on the spot. A typical one was; 'I saw a female, solitary, brooding. Who is she?' They suggested various women from myth and history, Helen or Cleopatra, but no one thought of 'a hen'.

Another one posed was, 'It runs over fields and woods all day, under the bed at night sits not alone, with long tongue hanging out, a-waiting for a bone.'

They suggested 'a dog', 'a wolf', 'a mouse' and all sorts but no one suggested 'a shoe'.

They came, they listened and they answered but nobody got even two questions right. They didn't get as far as the task and they were thrown out on their noses. Not one of them was good enough for her. The King of Canterbury sent word the length and breadth of the land for suitors and eventually it came to the ears of the King of Northumbria.

Now, the King of Northumbria had three sons. The eldest two were fine, strapping young princes; they found royal living easy for they rode well, hunted with the best and caroused long into the night with song and wine. But the youngest son was different; Jack, a very clever lad. As soon as he could talk he could outwit his two brothers. All very well, but one day, when he made even the King look foolish, it was one step too far. The King commanded that if Jack were to stay in the castle he would live with the Royal Jester and be dressed in motley, the two-coloured rags of professional idiots, and wear a long pointed hood with floppy ears and a tassel. He would never be treated as a prince, only as a fool.

Yet he lived as a court jester quite happily. He learned magic tricks, juggling, song, storytelling and jokes. The Queen did what she could to make his life easy and, although he often had fun at the King's expense, there was always a nugget of wisdom in the jest.

The King gathered his sons together and told them the news about the marriageable princess in Canterbury.

This made the eldest prince quite excited. 'The Kingdom of Kent is the richest in the land. I shall go there at once and win her hand, for I always win all contests; riding, swordplay or fist.'

The second prince objected. 'But I think that she should marry me. As eldest son you will inherit the whole Kingdom of Northumbria when father dies but I shall have nothing. By strength and courage I shall win the Princesses hand.'

Jack the Fool said, 'The contest is one of wit, not strength nor courage. I hear that she will ask three questions and even if you can answer them you will be set a task to carry out. Now, if you really wish to appear clever – take me with you. If you are compared with me you will seem to be the cleverest in the land.'

The King demanded that they take Jack with them; after all it was a long journey and with any luck he would get lost.

So it was that the three brothers set off for Canterbury on horseback. Well, actually two horses and a donkey. They made good time except that Jack would stop for anything that took his eye. Some bird's eggs were taken from a nest on an overhanging branch and stored carefully in the capacious pockets of his motley. A distorted hazel branch made him call out, 'Look at this mystery, brothers,' but they were anxious to get to Canterbury and urged him to hurry on. He stored the branch deep in his motley. He stopped to pick up hazel nuts which he chewed on the way. He was so slow that the brothers were close to leaving him behind and they would have done so but for what their mother would say.

After two weeks riding they came to Canterbury Castle. The two eldest brothers had picked great bunches of flowers for the Princess and took them to the Royal Reception Room after dressing in their finest clothes and practicing their winning smiles. Jack gambolled along behind them in his usual motley. With respectfully downcast eyes they solemnly presented the flowers to the Princess who was sat on her throne, but she didn't even glance at them. She was distracted by the whirling yellow and red of something somersaulting across the marble floor towards her and ending up in a heap at her royal feet. Jack looked at her straight in the eyes and said, 'Hello, m'dear.'

Jack's brothers tried to apologise for Jacks' boldness but the Princess ignored them. She was not used to such a direct gaze. His eyes were penetrating but warm. She blushed, looked directly back at Jack and asked, 'What are you looking at? And for goodness sake do not say 'Your extraordinary beauty, my Lady' like all the others or I will have your head removed.'

'I am looking at your chest, my Lady,' replied Jack. The Princess was wearing a low-cut dress; her cleavage shimmered above the brocade. 'It looks hot enough to hatch my eggs.' He drew an egg from his pocket.

The Princess started to shake. She was trying to maintain her haughty appearance but Jack had made her giggle. She spluttered, 'And how would you retrieve such an egg from my bosom, my lad?'

'Why, I have the tool right here,' said Jack as he withdrew the curled hazel branch from his clothes. The Princess laughed aloud.

'And how do you happen to have a great branch in your possession?' Jack brought out a handful of hazel nuts and showed them to the Pincess.

'I always keep a nut. A nut will produce a shoot, the shoot shall become a root, the root will grow into a tree and the tree will bear a branch. Now that is three questions asked and three answered. I therefore claim you as my bride.'

The King of Canterbury hurried down the stairs from the balcony where he had been keeping an eye on the proceedings. His daughter marrying a fool? What nonsense was this? The King's voice boomed out, 'You seem to forget, you idiot, that a task must be done. On this occasion I shall set the task, as the future of my kingdom shall rest upon the result. In one month's time you shall return here and sit with the Princess all night without a blink of sleep. Do that and your marriage with be assured.'

'And if I should sleep? What then?' smiled Jack.

'If your eyes close even once then off shall come your silly head,' roared the King.

'Fair enough,' grinned Jack, 'for you would be doing my father a favour. He has had my head hidden in this jesters' hood for many long years.'

The three brothers rode back to Northumbria; it took two more weeks. As soon as they had all arrived Jack said, 'Well, I must be off back to Canterbury again for my task, it is a fortnights' journey.' He mounted his donkey and again rode south.

Jack would still stop for anything that took his interest. As he crossed a stream he noticed shoals of silvery fish swimming below. He scooped some up and put them into his motley pockets. He dallied and wandered but he arrived in Canterbury just in time to perform the King of Canterbury's task.

A great banquet had been prepared for the Princess and Jack. Beef pies, sausages, stuffed rabbits and cream-filled pastries; sumptuous fruit fools with thick cream; rich heavy foods with soporific wines and ales all ordered by the King and chosen to make Jack sleepy. A fool for a son-in-law indeed! Ridiculous! He had just the place for the head of a fool – up on a spike on the Westgate Towers.

The great dining table groaned with the weight of the feast but only the two were there to eat it. As the evening progressed the Princess pecked at tiny mouthfuls but Jack had plates piled high with food and seemed to drink many glasses of wine. The meal went on late into the night with many friendly words and laughter between the diners. As the cathedral bells chimed the midnight hour the Princess noticed Jack's head resting on the table as if he were about to fall asleep. She gave him a great nudge with her elbow and said, 'Wake up, Jack, if you close your eyes my father will have your head off!'

Now Jack was not really that sleepy. Most of the food he had seemed to eat and all of the wine had been slipped into his motley pockets. He pretended to wake with a snort and said, 'Fear not, my lovely, I was not sleeping but concentrating on my fishing.'

'Your fishing? You are far from water here; the Stour flows outside the castle, not in it. There are no fish to be caught. I am very much afraid, my darling, that you were dreaming.'

'Then what is this?' said Jack producing a silvery fish from his pocket, then another and another. 'Are these not a fine catch?'

The Princess started to giggle. 'And not only silver fish to be caught,' continued Jack, 'but sausage-fish and plumb-fish too.' Out came what he had not eaten at table. The Princess laughed loudly and put her fond arms round his neck.

'But you must be tired after your long journey. You may sleep if you wish to and I shall wake you if my father comes.' She took off his fool's hood, smoothed his hair and kissed him. 'I shall keep you safe,' she whispered, 'for you shall be my love.'

The King of Canterbury and his men burst into the dining hall at dawn to find Jack with his head on the table and his eyes closed.

'So, he sleeps as I knew he must," crowed the King, 'take him to the yard and remove his head.'

'No, no,' cried the Princess, 'he is not asleep but listening for fish. There are many to be caught here – he has been catching them all night. Have you not Jack?' She shook him and he woke up. 'Are you not fishing, Jack?'

'And where in this room would you find a fish to catch,' snorted the King.

Jack blinked a little and palmed a couple of fish from his pocket into his hand. Now would be a good time to use the conjuring he had learned from the Royal Jester at home. He walked right up to the King and said, 'In this season the fish are to be found in royal pockets.'

He reached into the King's best embroidered hunting jacket pocket and pulled out a flapping fish. 'And swimming in the crown,' he said, producing another from behind the King's head. The King was amazed and pleased and amused. He clapped Jack on the back and called him a fine fellow.

A month later, dressed in royal clothes, looking so fine that his brothers scarcely recognised him, he was married to the Princess. They lived happily together in Canterbury for many years and the motley hung in the back of his wardrobe to remind him, every morning when he dressed, the wisdom of being a fool.

Ten

THE BATTLE
OF SANDWICH

Perhaps it seems odd to put the words 'Sandwich' and 'Battle' together in the same sentence? How can these two words go together unless we picture the air full of flying cucumber on thin slices of brown bread? Chip butties being thrown with deadly accuracy? The answer is that the town of Sandwich used to be one of the largest, busiest ports in England until the river Stour silted up, taking the sea a winding 2 miles away.

It was the fault of those rotten monks from Minster and Canterbury; they were given the land around the Wantsum Channel by the local leader and Sandwich resident King Canute; which divided the Isle of Thanet from the rest of Kent. They ploughed and this loosened the soil which washed into the river with every rain. The people complained about it to the first Queen Elizabeth when she visited the town but after a bit of swearing from one of the local ladies she became a little grumpy and had no more to do with them. Until then Sandwich had been a busy Cinque Port, one of the places that had been chosen to supply naval defences for the English Channel coast in return for exemptions from various laws, tolls and taxes.

It was the town's position on the east-facing coast that had made them successful. The prevailing wind is from the south-west which is fine for sailing north up the Channel but until sailors learned to tack against the wind they had to wait for a northerly breeze to blow them south. This meant many ships and their crews were moored for weeks off the 'Downs' in Sandwich Haven, waiting for the right wind. The townspeople supplied them with everything that they wanted or needed; ropes, sails, ship repairs, food, drink and women. The supply of ladies explains the curious naming of the narrow Sandwich streets still called 'Paradise Row' and 'Love Lane'.

Anyway, when the barons, who had signed the Magna Carta, found that King John was going back on the agreement, they went to the French King Philip's son, Louis of France, for support. Louis needed little excuse to invade and soon Louis and his fleet were in Sandwich, which they sacked and burnt like most of the other Cinque Ports. He then went to London, assumed the crown, had a bit of civil war trouble and was soon sending to France for more supplies and men. Kent was mainly taken over by the French but Dover Castle was defended by Hubert de Burgh. Dover and its castle were seen as the 'Clavis Angliae', the lynchpin of the English defences.

On 24 August, 1217, around eighty French ships were seen in the Straits of Dover and Hubert de Burgh set sail with a fleet of only thirty ships from Dover to see them off. This French fleet was full of soldiers, horses and sailors and was lead by Eustace, the mad monk. Eustace was a pirate and a good sailor. Although he had once been a Benedictine monk he had also studied the 'Black Arts' at Toledo in Spain. He was, it was said, a wizard.

Hubert de Burgh was a better sailor than the French commander and he knew the Dover Straits well. Not only that but he also sailed upwind of the enemy and threw powdered quicklime into the air, blinding the French sailors. Soon many of the French fleet had been sunk, burned or seized.

Now, Eustace and ten other ships of his fleet headed up north towards Sandwich and the Wandsum Channel as a short cut to London. They met Philippe d'Aubigney in charge of the English fleet off Sandwich Haven. Not much of a fleet; only three small ships.

But they were crewed by local men who knew the currents and sandbanks well. Amongst them was their secret weapon, Stephen Crabbe of Sandwich. He was not only a skilled sailor but he, too, had studied the 'Black Arts' in Toledo.

The three small boats had another advantage. The French ships were 'cogs' and had tall superstructures on the prow and stern, including even taller catapults for throwing rocks at castles, which made them liable to capsize in gusty weather. The English men prayed to St Bartholomew (it being his Saint's Day) for aid. 'Give us a hand,' they said, 'and we vow we'll build you a chapel.' A small, local storm obligingly started up and half a dozen of the French ships capsized. Some say that a figure in a red robe was seen floating in the skies above.

As the two opposing forces sailed closer to each other something strange was seen; or rather not seen. Stephen Crabbe was sure that the French had possessed eleven boats; six had sunk but now he counted only four. The ship that carried the mad monk was missing.

Where was he? Here the magical training Stephen had learned in Toledo became useful.

He reached into his pouch and brought out a piece of blue Spanish glass. He put it to his eye and through it he could see Eustace's ship with the mad monk standing in the prow. He blinked and lowered the glass. Without the glass there was nothing to see.

The other Sandwich men were surprised when Stephen manoeuvred their boat to a stretch of empty water, leapt off their deck and into clear air. He did not fall into the sea but with the blue glass held to his eye with one hand and a sword in the other he slashed at invisible enemies whilst floating yards above the waves. Eustace, astounded to be seen, ran away and hid in the bowels of the ship but Stephen quickly found him and cut off his head. The French crew now recovered their courage and, outnumbered, Stephen Crabbe was hacked to pieces, which were thrown into the sea. But as Eustace died the French ship had re-appeared and the Kentish lads soon seized the boat.

The rest of the French fleet was soon defeated and Eustace's head was paraded on a spear around Dover and Canterbury. The men of Sandwich kept their word and if you visit Sandwich on 24 August you can watch children racing around St Bart's Chapel to win a bun. And now you can tell them why they are doing it.

Eleven

THE HAND OF GLORY

The population of any city changes over the weeks, the months and the years. Once or twice a week markets swell the roads with traffic; in each season festivals fill the air with flags and music whilst colleges and universities close their doors and the students travel home or abroad. Several hundred years ago all this applied to Canterbury, but even more so. Canterbury was, and still is, a favourite destination for pilgrims. On high days and holy days the streets would be crowded with pilgrims keen to visit the tomb of Thomas Becket the Martyr. Not only for the good of their souls but to buy tiny bottles of 'Beckets Blood', said to cure blindness, epilepsy and leprosy.

The crowds were huge and everyone needed somewhere to stay. Alehouses were full; inns were packed with people. Hostels increased their capacity by resting wooden planks across the narrow medieval streets to borrow upper rooms from private houses across the road. The Eastbridge Hospital in the High Street was often packed with soldiers back from the wars as well as the usual pilgrims. Canterbury would be full to bursting.

The Sun Inn near the Cathedral gate was amongst those that had expanded to take in more travellers. Wattle and daub walls were knocked through to neighbouring houses up and down Sun Street whilst back yards behind the houses and shops in nearby Guildhall Street were roofed in canvas to create more rooms.

One Easter the Sun Inn was packed full of 'regulars' and visitors. The public bar was heaving with customers; the air was full of smoke, song, curses and conversation. Yet through this packed throng darted a tiny childlike figure, as easily as a minnow amongst riverweeds. Dark, curly hair and quick brown eyes; she was Alise, the potgirl. She was not a child, for if you looked into her face you would see that it was mature and intelligent. She could fill and refill tankards and glasses with wine, brandy or beer and keep a note of precisely who had drunk and eaten what. A small worn slate hung from her waist, covered in chalk tallies. A note of these would be given to the landlord as the customer left. Yet not a word was ever spoken, for Alise was a mute. It was said that she had been found in the bilges of a ship from the Low Countries, perhaps as a refugee from religious persecution.

As the evening grew late many tired pilgrims retired to their beds. The musician wrapped his hurdy-gurdy in a cloth and put his pipes in his bag. Card games were finished, scraps from the plates were thrown into the street for the pigs to eat and drunkards were woken and sent to their homes. The landlord counted his takings at the long table. The great fire burnt low in the enormous fireplace and Alise swept the floor before she retired to the warm hollow in the bricks beside the chimney where she slept behind a thick curtain. A clock chimed midnight in the echoing streets. A soft tapping came from the street door and the landlord shouted, 'No room, all beds taken, try the Hospital by the bridge on the High Street.'

The tapping came again. A muffled voice cried, 'They are full too. I need little space for I am thin and very old. Have mercy on an old dame. I do have a little money.' The word 'money' stirred the landlord and he swept all his takings into his leather pouch and unbolted the heavy door to see who this stranger could be.

The lamplight showed a frail old woman in long skirts and with lank grey hair. 'I have some coppers and would be satisfied to sleep on the floor. I will take up no room at all.' She held out a thick-wristed hand holding a few coins. The landlord glanced down. Three copper coins lay in the dirty palm, but a small tarnished silver coin was almost invisible beneath them. 'I suppose I must be charitable,' muttered the landlord holding out his hand for the money, 'come in and stay by the fire.' The coins were tipped into his hand and the crone tottered over the threshold. The landlord couldn't stop himself grunting with satisfaction; with the silver coin she was unknowingly paying more than she would for a room and yet she would sleep on the floor. He took himself off down the road to his bed. The inn grew quiet.

Alise heard all this from her pallet in the niche behind the curtain. The old woman had sounded – wrong. Alise may never have spoken but she could hear and listen very well. That was no woman's voice, she thought. Alise opened the curtain a crack and peeped through. She could see the old woman violently scratching her head, her fingers dislodging the greasy grey wig that covered her short black hair. The man, for now she could see through the disguise it was obvious that he was a man, reached into his shoulder bag and withdrew a cloth-wrapped object. Then out came a small metal plate with a spike in the centre. The cloth was unfolded to reveal a mummified left hand, shrunken and grey-green. The man stood the hand on the plate with the fingers pointing upwards and produced a taper. This he lit from the embers of the fire and touched a flame to each finger of the hand. Three fingers and the thumb sported blue flames but the little finger refused to light.

The man cursed softly. Twice more he tried to ignite the finger but it remained unlit. Alise was scared. He was so close to her. He had only to pull back the curtain to find her. The man's voice was speaking. In low tones he recited, 'Serpens nequissimus, let all those who are asleep remain asleep, let those who are awake remain awake.'

But I am awake, thought Alise; maybe that is why the little finger will not light. The man took off his long ragged skirt showing heavy boots and knee-length trousers and took his shoulder bag to the stairs door on the opposite side of the fireplace. With no attempt at stealth he mounted the creaky steps to the bedrooms above. What could a small person like Alise do? She could not scream. If she did nothing they would all be robbed in their bewitched sleep. She

slipped silently from behind the curtain and stepped up to the burning hand.

Was the enchantment in the flames? They seemed an unearthly colour and Alise felt no heat coming from them. Upstairs the sound of the thief's boots were loud on the bare floorboards as he moved from room to room taking what he wanted. Alise blew on the flames but was surprised to see that they did not extinguish, rather they burned brighter than before. She tried pinching them out but the blue fire seemed to wriggle over the skin of her hand and back to the hair-like wick. A neglected wineglass stood on the windowsill with an inch of murky liquid in the bottom. Alise sniffed it; slops of French wine by the smell of it. She threw it over the hand and a flash like gunpowder was the result. Both beer and water from the jug had the same explosive effect.

What about the landlord? Perhaps she could wake the landlord. He had let out his fine bedroom upstairs to a bishop and he himself slept in a tiny room over the apothecary shop four doors up the road. Maybe the sleeping spell had not reached him there. Alise tried to slide the street door bolts back quietly but the bottom bolt was stiff and shot back with a bang. She froze but soon heard the continued scuffling from above as the thief rifled the rooms. Being so small she could only reach the top bolt by climbing up and balancing on the thick batten that held the vertical planks. The top bolt slid easily and she was soon running up the street to the apothecary shop and banging on the door. Twice she knocked but no one came. She knew that the apothecary drank heavily and that the landlord always had a large glass of brandy when the takings had been counted. It would be difficult to wake them even without the spell.

The answer must lie in the flaming hand. As she returned to the inn she noticed a saucer of 'blue milk', the squeezings from a cheese press, on a windowsill where foraging pigs could not reach it. The weaver's cat could do without it for once, thought Alise. She carried it carefully to the inn, silently opened the door and approached the burning 'Hand of Glory'. The blue glow diminished as the milk grew nearer. Encouraged, Alise threw the contents of the saucer over the hand.

The flames died immediately and acrid green smoke curled upwards. There were shouts from above as people awoke,

'Thief, thief, seize him, he has my purse!' and 'Catch him, some one, do not let him escape.' There were the sounds of running bare feet pursuing boots, a heavy body crashing to the floor spilling coins and treasure across the boards. She could hear a rattle of boots clattering down the steep winding stairs. The stairs door burst open and there was the thief, wild eyed and desperate. Alise opened her mouth to scream but, of course, no noise came forth. He hesitated, looking from the street door to the Hand of Glory, seemingly unable to choose between the safety of escape and the loss of the hand. As the landlord appeared at the street door a burly pilgrim ran down the stairs. The thief was trapped, seized, bound and put into the cellar to be dealt with in the morning.

The thief was put to death outside the city walls and his body gibbeted as an example to others. Much money and many valuables were recovered from his hiding place in Rough Common above the city. The Hand of Glory was exorcised and burned.

What happened to Alise is not recorded but I have heard that in a castle in South Kent, prized for its collection of Samurai armour, there is a glass case full of what may seem to be dolls clothes and shoes; all exquisitely made in half human size and covered in jewels and gold thread. The name on the faded label reads 'Alise Knopf'. Maybe these beautiful clothes were made for Alise as a reward.

Twelve

PULLING GAME

About half a dozen pretty miles south west of Canterbury is the village of Chilham, complete with its own castle. When our story starts, around 1200, the castle was occupied by Fulbert de Lucy's family who lived there, by the King's grace, for 250 years.

The castle consisted of three baileys, a barbican gate and 8 acres of land. Adjoining them were the 'King's Woods'; a wonderful place for the Royal hunting of boar and deer. Now in those days the peasants were poor and fresh meat was a rarity; so poaching in these woods was rife. Many a lowly cottage fire cooked a stolen rabbit; a crafty partridge added to the pottage or a roast boar piglet would be a welcome treat for anyone. It always tasted better when stolen, you see.

But deer was the most coveted prize. One early morning Boswell and Cox, two local lads, had hunted and killed an enormous red deer. He was a 'hart of ten'; he had that many branches on his antlers and was more than five years old. The buck had lead them a long way through the dense woods but at last an bolt from Boswell's crossbow had taken him cleanly in the neck and he had eventually collapsed with a last sigh. He was huge. Now they needed to get the great animal back to their cart. Here was meat for as much as two months; deerskin for shoes and antlers for knife handles. He was a solid animal with wide spreading antlers. How would they get him to the cart? They tried lifting him onto their shoulders but he was just too heavy. Boswell said, 'We must drag the animal. With the dew still on the ground he will slide well.'

'The antlers look lighter than the haunches. We should pull them,' said Cox.

'Quite right,' replied Boswell, 'which way is it to the cart?'

'That way,' pointed Cox.

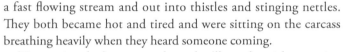

They pulled and they tugged the game through ferns and brambles. For two hours they struggled between trees and bushes, up and down slopes, through a fast flowing stream and out into thistles and stinging nettles. They both became hot and tired and were sitting on the carcass breathing heavily when they heard someone coming.

'Keep quiet, don't move; perhaps they'll pass by without seeing us,' whispered Cox. The punishments for poaching were severe; you could lose your freedom, a hand or even your life for stealing from the King's hunting forests. The pair watched carefully between the fern fronds and saw a short peasant woman come into view. Her back was bent, her head was down and she was pulling a large stag behind her and moving pretty fast.

She didn't see them until they stood up in the ferns and called to her, 'Greetings,' called Cox, 'do not be alarmed. We are not verderers but lads out hunting as you are. A fine venison you have there.'

She turned and looked at them with a scowl. 'And what do you want with me, boys? Think you can take my meat? I killed this great beast with my own hands; do you think I would let it go easily? Look, my knife is long and sharp.' She pulled a vicious-looking cleaver from under her cloak.

'No, no, you do us wrong,' called Boswell, 'we have meat of our own, a fine stag nearly as big as yours. But answer me this; how can a woman as small as you move so quickly and easily with such a heavy burden? We are two strong lads yet we cannot travel as fast as you with our prey.'

'Let's look at your animal,' replied the woman, 'bring it out here.'

Boswell and Cox struggled with the horns to pull the beast through the undergrowth. Eventually it was on the path. The short lady walked round it and lifted one of the back legs, weighed it in her hand and dropped it. She lifted the head and examined the antlers which were tangled with twigs and ferns. Then she walked around the lads and regarded them with a critical eye.

'Right,' she said, 'your animal is no larger than mine. You are both strong, healthy boys. But you are not using your heads.' Boswell and Cox stared at her; then at each other. Cox put his hands to his head and looked at the stag. 'Is there then some clever way of using our heads to magic this beast back to our cart?' Boswell asked.

'Think, you numbskulls, think! That is how to use your heads. Why do you think there are plants around the horns of your deer?'

'They have gathered as we pulled it along, more and more. Those antlers catch on every branch, every root and every tussock of grass. They dig into the ground. We spend as much time pulling it free as pulling it along.'

The old woman's voice was scornful, 'And how was I pulling mine?'

'You were pulling it by – the – back – legs,' stumbled Boswell. 'Oh – I see. So the antlers didn't catch on the stuff and it slid easier. Cox; you are a loghead. It was you who suggested that we pull by the antlers; all this way we have sweated and groaned. Thank you dear lady, we now knows what to do.'

The woman watched them as they walked to the back of the stag, took a back leg each and dragged the animal a few paces.

'And don't you go scaring any more honest poachers,' the woman screeched.

'We shall not,' chorused the lads.

For two hours they struggled into thistles and stinging nettles, through a fast flowing stream, up and down slopes, in and out between trees and bushes. They had been pulling the stag for most of the afternoon when Cox said, 'Should we not have reached the cart by now?' Boswell looked at Cox with tired eyes. He was exhausted.

'Now we are using our heads it will take much longer. Since we started to pull the legs we have been moving further from the cart with every pace. The legs were pointing away from the cart, you see,' Boswell replied.

'Still, it is a lot easier, isn't it?'

'I suppose it is, my friend, I suppose it is.'

I don't know if they ever reached the cart.

Thirteen

NELL COOK AND THE DARK PASSAGE

Living in the precincts of Canterbury Cathedral, many years ago, there was a plump friar. He enjoyed the pleasures of life to an almost irreligious degree, especially food. Living there with him in his house was his servant, whose real name was Ellen Bean but was appreciatively called 'Nell Cook' by the friar.

Nell was a wonderful cook; she could take the cheapest cut of meat, the scrawniest rabbit or the rankest fish and make a meal that beguiled the nose, teased the tongue and satisfied the stomach. The friar grew fat and happy while Nell was content to serve him. The markets of Canterbury and the quay at Sandwich provided spices and herbs from as far away as Venice, Constantinople and Spain. Oils came from Greece, flours from Flanders, exotic vegetables from Africa and dried fruit from furthest India. All were blended and baked, filleted and fried, sauced and sliced into mouth-watering dishes. Every appetite of the friar was fulfilled by clever Nell.

The other friars of the Priory of St Saveur were a little critical of him; there seemed to be rather too much indulgence for a man of the cloth. Yet he did his duties and attended all the services and nothing was said.

All went well until the friar announced that there would soon be one more person living with them. His brother was a sea captain, he said, and was due to travel far across the oceans for two or three years. His brother's daughter, his niece, would be taking over the top bedroom until the captain returned. She was, apparently, a good modest church-going girl who spent most of her time sewing, praying or singing hymns.

Now Nell had never heard the friar mention a brother before but she prepared the room and a bed as instructed. However, when the girl arrived she did not seem to be much of a holy person at all. She skipped merrily everywhere letting her legs show and bending forward in her low-cut bodice. Her songs were not those of the church but of the alehouse; no hymns of praise but rude ditties of lusty maids and sailors, of milkmaids and shepherds. Nell did not warm to her at all. Her murmured close conversations with the friar made Nell's blood seethe; their laughter while playing cards made her grind her teeth.

However, one thing roused Nell's suspicion the most, for the girls bed was never slept in. Every morning Nell would toil up the narrow stairs with fresh water for the jug and every morning she would find the bed as she had left it the morning before. The chamber pot under the bed had never been used. Either the girl was very neat and tidy, making the bed when she rose, or, much more likely, the bed was not slept in at all. If that were the case, thought Nell, where was she sleeping? The house door to the Cathedral Precinct was locked every night and was still found fastened securely every morning. The window in the top room gave onto a sheer drop of forty feet, no way out there.

Nell had to know. She took the poker and the tongs from the fireplace in the kitchen and laid them under the bottom sheet of the girl's bed. Now she must complain of an uncomfortable night's sleep and if she didn't , well … , thought Nell.

Three days went by and not a word of complaint or discomfort from the girl. The next night Nell did not sleep but rose in the early hours of the morning and crept up to the friar's room. The door was very old and warped, leaving a narrow crack between the planks.

Nell put her eye to the gap. Pink shapes were bouncing around in the bedroom; giggles and squeals came through the door. Nell's face darkened, blood suffused her neck and her eyes turned red. This cannot go on, she thought. Something must be done.

Early the next morning Nell passed through the Cathedral Gate into the Buttermarket. She crossed the road to the apothecary shop and bought a bottle of the most powerful poison, saying that there were vermin in the friar's house that must be removed. Nell smiled a wicked smile. Human vermin, she thought.

Nell made her most famous dish, Warden Pie. This she usually made of whatever was kept or caught in the Cathedral Precincts. Rabbit, sparrow, thrush, mouse; all were cleverly prepared and encased in a deep raised pastry case. Today she had pigeon and rabbit, which she broiled with onions and sauced adding three spoonfuls of green poison to the mix. A crisp crust of pastry enclosed it all with a bird and a rabbit drawn into the crust on the top. The next morning the steaming pie was put outside the friar's bedroom door and the fragrance wafted through the crack in the wood.

The friar was not particularly missed at Lauds, the dawn service; he had often been late recently giving the excuse of a bad headache. But at the next service, Prime, the other priests did wonder where he was and in the evening after Vespers they politely knocked on the door of his house. Nell answered with a questioning look, saying

truthfully that she had been at the market since early morning and had not seen the friar at all that day. She showed the priests up to the bedroom where they were surprised to find the door barred from the inside. They could see shapes through the crack that were two bare bodies on the bed. When there was no response to their pounding they broke down the door and discovered the friar and his niece in an embarrassing position and both stone dead. Their tongues were black and protruding from their mouths; their eyes were open and staring. A pie with two bites missing rested on the niece's voluptuous chest.

Now nobody likes a scandal. The more respected you are the less you like it. The Church thought itself very well respected; there could be no scandal. The friar was buried in the Cathedral grounds with due ceremony as all servants of the church were. No mention was ever made of the 'niece' and her body simply disappeared. Nell Cook also disappeared.

That is, until a couple of hundred years later when three masons started restoration work round to the left of St Adhelm's Tower. When the pavement was restored between the old infirmary cloister and the Green Court in the time of Dean Bargrave a stone was lifted to reveal a hollow space containing the emaciated corpse of a middle-aged woman and the desiccated remains of a pie with three bites taken from it. It seems that the friars could not put Nell to death; it went against their vows, but they could leave her in a situation where she could choose to starve or eat the poisoned pie.

Within a year the three masons were dead. Two were hung at Tyburn for the murder of the third. From that moment on visitors to the Cathedral on a Friday evening would hear unearthly screams coming from what is now known as the Dark Passage. It was said that anyone who heard that scream would die within the year.

The rumour about the scream killing people is, of course, nonsense. I myself heard that scream eleven months ago and noth ....aghaghhhhh.

Fourteen

THE THREE FEATHERS

It seems that in the olden days, when fish flew and pigs played bagpipes, there was a very old Kentish King. He was frail and weak and did not know which of his three sons should inherit his kingdom. Obviously not the simpleton, who was a long streak of nothing, but the other two princes were equal; in strength, courage and looks. He decided that he would set all three a task; the simpleton would, of course, fail but it would help the King to choose between the other two.

The King summoned his sons to the road outside the castle gate. In a quivery tone he said, 'My boys, one of you must become King when I die. To help me to choose between you there will be a test. You must go abroad in the land to find a carpet; a carpet of the finest wove. The one who brings back the best will rule the land.'

He held high his hand which was holding three feathers; from an owl, a goose and a wren. 'Now, I shall have no fighting or stealing between you. Each of you will choose a feather. When the wind takes these plumes you will follow where they go to find your fortunes. Which do you choose, eldest son?'

The young prince thought hard. He wouldn't want to travel very far; in his opinion this was all a waste of effort. Whichever of the two elder brothers found the best carpet would win, share the fortune and rule together with his brother. As long as the simpleton was shown to lose, that was the important thing.

'The owls feather for me, father.'

'And middle son, which feather for you?' the King queried.

The middle son was fit and strong and chose the wren's feather. He could do with a long run. Who cared if his brother won? The simpleton would lose whatever happened.

'The tiny wren shall be my guide.'

This left the simpleton with no choice but the goose feather. The King held his hand high in the breeze. He pursed his wrinkled lips, blew and let the feathers go. The wren feather was wafted to the east and bobbed over the pastures with the middle prince running behind. His bright red jacket became a dot in the landscape.

The owl feather fell nearly to the ground before floating upwards and away to the west. The eldest prince watched it go then calmly walked after it. The heavy goose feather fell straight to the ground.

The simpleton looked at it for a moment in despair. He sank to his heels then sat on the ground. How would he follow this feather to a beautiful carpet if it didn't go anywhere? The King walked back into the castle.

The simpleton stared at the feather resting on the stone. He saw that under the feather was a straight crack. His eye followed along the crack a yard then a corner appeared. Then another crack, another yard and then another corner. Then two more. Brushing a little soil from a hollow between his feet revealed a grey metal ring. He was sitting on a stone trapdoor.

Well, he thought, this is where the feather landed. This must be where to find a carpet. He looped his fingers through the iron ring and pulled. At first nothing happened but suddenly with a cracking sound the trapdoor sprang open. As the dust cleared the simpleton could see a set of stone steps leading down below. He laid the trapdoor back and started to lower himself into the hole. The steps were worn and smooth, becoming damp as he descended. He came to a mouldy wooden door and being a polite lad he knocked on it.

Through the door he heard a deep liquid voice singing:

> ♪ Little green maiden small ♪
> Hop across the slippery floor
> See who's knocking at the door
> ♪ Bring him in to meet us all ♪

The door opened and there before him was a small green toad. She held out a webbed hand and led him in. Beyond was a small damp cave with a huge fat yellow toad sitting on a smelly cushion and wearing a thin golden crown. She was surrounded by dozens of little green toads. The huge fat toad spoke in oily words, 'Welcome, Prince, to our webbed queendom. Why have you come and what do you seek?'

'Well,' said the simpleton. He was a bit startled to be reminded that he was a prince, for as long as he could remember everyone had called him the simpleton. 'I don't suppose you have a beautiful carpet handy, do you?' He looked around the wet cave doubtfully.

The huge fat toad leaned her wide head back and sang:

> ♪ Little green maiden small ♪
> Slide and slip and slither
> Bring the great box thither
> ♪ And open it withal ♪

The tiny green toad hopped off and after a moment came struggling back carrying a long wooden box. She opened the box to reveal the most ornate, finely woven carpet ever seen. It glowed with deep reds, vibrant greens and bright blues, interwoven with threads of silver and gold.

'This is yours, oh prince,' burbled the Toad Queen.

The simpleton thanked the toads and took the carpet over his shoulder through the door, up the stone steps and back to the world above. There he met his brothers who had not bothered to look very far and who carried only a fireside rug and a doormat. They each carried their prizes into the castle to show to the King.

The King naturally declared the simpleton the winner as soon as he saw his carpet. This came as a terrible shock to the two older princes and they protested at the tops of their voices. How could the King ever put a simpleton in charge of a whole kingdom? Didn't the King realise that things come in threes in stories? He should set another challenge.

They made so much noise that the King eventually declared another quest. This time they must follow the feathers to find the finest, most valuable ring in the land. Once again they assembled outside the castle and again the King blew the feathers into the air.

The owl feather blew straight over his shoulder and up and over the castle. The eldest prince strolled to the stables, mounted his stallion and trotted off round the castle walls. The wren feather floated away towards the distant hills beyond the woods. The middle prince ran fast and true through the woods and disappeared towards the hills. The red speck of his jacket could be seen moving up the far slopes. The heavy goose feather fell straight to the ground.

The simpleton looked at the feather and then at the King. He asked, 'Father, did I have a name when I was born? Did my mother call me simpleton when I came into this world?'

The King looked at him thoughtfully. He had to think hard but at last it came to his mind from many years before. 'I seem to remember that the Queen named you on the day that you were born, the very day she died. She said, 'Call him Jack.' But your eyes were crossed and your tongue lolled out so we called you Simpleton. And so it stayed for all these years.'

'Jack is a fine name, father. Thank you, I shall use it from now on. Now I must find that precious ring.'

The King walked back into the castle and Jack found the iron ring of the trapdoor under the goose feather. He pulled the ring, lifted the door and descended the steps once again to the realm of the toads. He knocked on the mouldy door and listened. There was that liquid voice again:

♪ Little green maiden small ♪
Hop across the slippery floor
See who's knocking at the door
♪ Bring him in to meet us all ♪

The door was once again opened by the small green toad. There sat the Toad Queen on her moist cushion, her crown slightly tilted over her eye. She looked at him with an amphibian smile and asked, 'What do you seek this time, Prince Jack?'

'You know my name,' gasped Jack, 'how do you know my name when I have only just learned of it myself?'

'We toads know many things, Jack. Besides, I am not only the Queen of the Toads but also a sorceress. And I was under the bed when you were named. What do you seek this time?'

Jack thought that he must explain. 'My father, the King, is old and will soon die. He would want to leave the kingdom in strong wise hands and must choose between my brothers and myself. He set us the task of finding the most wonderful carpet and although mine was the best, thank you again for that, he has set us a new task – to find the finest, the most precious ring.'

The huge fat toad leaned her broad head back, opened her wide mouth and sang:

♪ Little green maiden small ♪
Slide and slip and slither
Bring the small box thither
♪ And open it withal ♪

This time the box the little green toad brought was small and deep red. When the Toad Queen opened it and took out an ornate ring

Jack was nearly blinded by the light that was reflected from the stone's facets. Vermillion and purple, saffron and turquoise, green and yellow sparkled from the stone whilst the ring shone gold with heavy intricate value.

'This is yours, oh Prince,' said the Toad Queen.

Jack thanked her, took it in his hand, climbed the stone stairs back to the world above and met his two brothers. Thinking that there was no real competition they had found a bronze ring from a horse harness and the broken rim of a brass candlestick. They all went to find the King. Once again Jack was declared the clear winner. The older princes were hopping with fury. They demanded that a further task should be set (reminding the King of the 'rule of three'), so the King said, 'This shall be your very last task. Go forth and follow your feathers to find the most beautiful woman in the land.'

The three feathers were held high and blown into the breeze. The owl feather flew east over fields and streams and combing his hair the eldest prince strolled after it. The wren feather headed west this time, towards the town. The middle prince ran after it in the short-sleeved leather jerkin that made his muscles look big. The town and country is full of pretty women for us brothers, he thought, but who would fancy a simpleton?

Jack once again lifted the stone slab and descended to the cave of the toads. The little toad led him by the hand to the Toad Queen. She sat on her soggy cushion with her crown over one eye like a pirate.

'Hail King Jack,' croaked the Queen, 'what do you seek in our noisome lair?'

'Well,' said Jack, 'it seems that these contests always come in threes. So I am not yet King Jack until I find the most beautiful woman in the land.' He looked around doubtfully. 'Do you get many beautiful women down here?'

'The most beautiful woman in the land? She is not here at the moment but will join us shortly. Take this to the Prince.'

She held out a yellow turnip to the small green toad who gave it to Jack. He looked at it; slightly mouldy and hollowed out with spiders webs dangling from the sides. He tried to look pleased. 'Lovely,' he said.

'And take these,' gargled the Queen.

She held four young mice in her webbed hand. The little green toad passed them across to Jack. The mice wriggled themselves into the tangle of cobwebs and stamped their tiny feet.

'Now take my daughter who answers the door and put her into the turnip.'

Jack carefully lifted the small green toad and placed her into the turnip. The turnip grew and transformed itself into a magnificent golden coach while the mice became four proud white stallions. The small green toad shook herself from head to webbed toe. Her green skin sloughed off and she grew into the most beautiful woman Jack had ever seen. He couldn't stop himself; he kissed her. He held her hand and gazed into her laughing eyes. He took her in his arms and squeezed her, thinking to himself that if he had done this a minute ago she would have shot out of his grip like a bar of wet soap.

Arm-in-arm they rode in that coach to the world above. They met his two brothers who had found some local peasant women. The brothers stared at the beautiful Toad Princess with their mouths hanging open. The women looked at her from the corners of their eyes and curled their lips. 'Hussy!' muttered one and the other whispered, 'No better than she should be.'

The three princes, their women and the King met in the great hall. Even with old, dim eyes the King could see who was the most beautiful. He declared that Jack should be the winner but the two older brothers shouted and swore, 'Another task, father, another task!' They looked round the hall for inspiration and noticed a chandelier hoop hanging from the ceiling by one chain.

'They should all leap though the hoop, father. The best should become queen.' The two local ladies would be sure to be fitter than a noble lady like the simpleton's choice, he thought.

The King furrowed his brow. 'But that then would be four tasks, one too many by your avowed custom.' But the two princes raved and made such a fuss ('If you really cared for the kingdom you would do it,' 'Do you love the simpleton more than us?') that the King relented.

The larger of the peasant ladies lined herself up, scraped her shoes on the floor, left right, left right, and then started to run towards the hoop. Unfortunately her shape was created by a corset, which sprang open as she ran and jumped. Her expanding body completely filled the iron ring and she stuck tight, arms waiving on one side and legs kicking on the other. It took two large servants, a jar of oil and two warmed spoons to get her out.

The other peasant lady tried but she was too long and thin to jump through cleanly. Her knees caught on the hoop and she spun over and over until her wig flew off and her false teeth shot out. When the servants untangled her she was a very sorry sight.

The Toad Princess was young, fit and, most importantly, a toad by upbringing. Toads can swim and croak but best of all they can hop and leap. She flew though the hoop effortlessly and was declared the winner.

The two princes and the peasant women left with sour expressions and were never seen again but Jack became King Jack and married the Toad Princess in great style; and he ruled the Kent kingdom with her for many forgotten years.

Fifteen

THE WANTSUM WYRM

If you were floating high above Kent you would see that the county forms the profile of a dog's faces gazing east out across the English Channel towards Belgium. Medway and the Isle of Grain form the eye and the ear and Folkstone forms the mouth. The nose is the Isle of Thanet. An Isle of Thanet, you ask? It is joined on to the rest of Kent quite firmly and any island must be, by definition, surrounded by water. So, how can Thanet be an island?

Well, if you could see back 2,000 years you would notice wide water between Sarre and Grove Ferry. The Wantsum Channel tides washed between Thanet and Kent twice a day. Used by the Romans and the Vikings, the French, the Venetians and the Dutch; it was an easier way to get to London than rounding Long Nose Spit and Margate Hook from Sandwich Haven. Safer despite the shallows and the tides in the Wantsum; from Reculver to Richborough there were always local people to 'help' if you were forced aground.

But where has it gone? Where is it now? What great convulsion of geology could remove a useful shortcut like that? Well, it wasn't geology, it was like this. Old fashioned mythology.

When the Isle of Thanet was an island King Phannit the Phirst ruled it. He was a good man and the proud father of a stunning daughter, Princess Phannetta. When she had passed sixteen summers he asked her whether she had yet found a spouse. He was so worried about it that he was chewing his beard. She was his only offspring, her mother was dead and if she didn't have more family the Isle of Thanet would fall into the hands of his brother, the King of Canterbury, when he died. The thought filled him with dread, so he organised great royal feasts where she could meet suitable princes.

Month after month the great banquets were given and Phannetta met many young men of royal blood. But she said no, none of them would do. All the princes around were wet or simple, she explained. Prince Chatham had floppy ears, Folkestone's breath smelled awful and Prince Rochester farted. None were good enough, although the King held wonderful feasts and dances for them all, from far and wide. Eventually he despaired of finding a prince, so he invited all the eligible young men and hired local musicians to play the wild dances that the common people preferred. The sonorous sounds of shrill pipes and deep bass drums filled the castle hall, shook the chalk of Phannit and thrummed below the Wantsum Channel where they woke the Wantsum Wyrm.

Now the Wantsum Wyrm was no garden animal, pink and brown and as long as your finger. He was a magical creature from the myths of time; he had once been the bane of the sailors of the northern seas but following a sorcerer's curse he had been asleep for 1,000 years. He was huge; he stretched from one end of the channel to the other in his underwater lair. When he awoke from the pounding of the drums he stretched his flaky scales, pushed his monstrous head above the waves and asked a passing farmer what all the noise was about. The farmer recovered his hat, which had flown off his head with the shock and haltingly told the Wyrm all about the Princess and her fussy tastes. The Wyrm knew that with his magical powers he could easily charm the Princess and he fancied a bit of royal luxury so he transformed himself into a well-dressed, handsome young prince and went to the party.

The Princess saw him and immediately fell in love. Well, he was bewitching, literally. She danced with him and no other until the early morning. I couldn't see from where I was standing but I expect they kissed. By the end of the night Princess Phannetta

told her father that she had found 'the one' that she would marry. King Phannit clapped his hands with delight and arranged their marriage for the next weekend. Hundreds of guests arrived over the next few days bringing gifts, food and wine. The wedding lasted three days and there was feasting, music and dancing late into the night.

Then it was the time. The newlywed couple climbed the stone stairs and went into the royal bedroom. They barred the door from inside and the King and the guests waited for the bloody sheet to be thrown out. This would prove that she had been a good girl in the past. They waited until breakfast then gave the door a gentle knock. No answer. The same happened at lunchtime and at supper; no answer. After three days they broke down the door with a battering ram to find an empty bedroom and the window flapping open.

Of course Prince Wyrm, having danced and eaten all night before his exhausting marital duties, had been worn out and fallen into a deep sleep. When he awoke he was hungry and forgetting that he was now a prince he had swallowed down the tasty naked pink Princess Phannetta whole. Then, realising what he had done and how annoyed the King would be, he had slithered out of the window and wriggled, as a Wyrm, down through the cabbage fields to the Wantsum Channel and deep below to his dank den.

King Phannit was hopping mad. 'I will give half my land and half my wealth to the one who finds my daughter and that prince,' he proclaimed. Well, they searched all the dwellings and the storehouses, up and down the Ramsgate cliffs and the Broadstairs beaches but nothing was found. A week went by. King Phannit began to despair.

'What shall I do now?' he wailed.

A little old man heard him and came forward. In a tremulous voice he said, 'In my Grandfather's time there was a man with such a fine nose that he could track a scent weeks after the quarry had gone.'

'Well, let that man be brought,' commanded the King.

Within three days a great snuffling noise was heard at the Folkstone Cliffs. People were astonished to see an enormous nose being pushed along on three wheelbarrows. It snuffled north, clearing the green cliffs of Dover as it went and leaving them chalky white, as you see them now. It sniffed up all the sand from the beaches of St Margaret's Bay, Kingsdown, Walmer, Deal and Sandwich leaving nothing but stones and shells, as you will find them today. The rest was sneezed out to sea forming the Goodwin Sands. The nose was ferried across the Wantsum Channel and taken to King Phannit's castle where it tracked the smell of the Princess all the way from the bedroom though the cabbages to the Wantsum shore where it said, 'I cannod track any furder, the tide has washed the scent away.'

'Oh, what shall I do now?' cried King Phannit.

The little old man said, 'Well, in my great-grandfather's time there was a man with a mouth and stomach so thirsty that he would drink not a gallon, not a pond but a whole sea in one gulp. He could certainly drink this lot.'

'Well, let that man be brought,' pleaded the King.

Within three days there was news of Lake Canterbury being drunk dry, Littlebourne Waters supped to a puddle, Wingham Well and Ash Pond licked to bare earth. When the great lips came to the Wantsum Channel they dipped and drank so deeply that soon fish were flapping on the greasy mud. Here was where the Wantsum Wyrm lived; a deep, dark slippery hole in the seabed. The King commanded that a soldier be armed with the sharpest weapons and be strongly armoured and then be lowered down the hole. When they pulled the rope up there was no soldier but a frayed end and a note from the Wyrm saying, 'Very tasty, thank you, but leave the shell off next time would you?'

'Oh, what on earth shall I do now?' moaned King Phannit.

The little old man said, 'Now, in my great-great-grandfather's time there was a man with fingers so strong and arms so long and so supple that he could reach down any hole and pull anything out.'

'Well, let that man be brought,' begged the King.

Within three days there was alarm around Chatham and Rochester as two great arms walked on ten great fingers and thumbs all along the north coast of Kent, a man balanced on them high above. You may see the great fingerprints today at Cliffe, Hoo, Upchurch and Kemsley. When the great hands reached Reculver they splashed through the mud, reached down the slippery hole and pulled out the great Wantsum Wyrm. The soldiers killed it, sliced it open and there was the princess – dead as a doornail.

'What, oh what shall I do now? She is dead,' cried King Phannit.

The little old man said, 'Do you know, in my great-great-great-grandfather's time there was a man with a black hat and a bottle of potion that could cure anything, even death.'

'Well, let that man be brought,' wailed the King.

The doctor was already there, so he sprinkled a little of the potion onto Phannetta's face and almost immediately she sat up and said, 'Hello Dad. I was gobbled up by a weird wyrm but I'm all right now. I shall marry the one who saved me. Who was it?'

The doctor with the bottle smiled a toothless smile and said, 'It was me, my dear, with my wonderful potion.'

'You could never have cured her down that hole,' said a voice from the top of the arms, 'I pulled the Wyrm out. I saved the princesses life. She should marry me.'

The great lips and stomach gurgled, 'And how could you have reached below the water? I drank the Wantsum dry. She should marry me.'

The huge nose sniffed. 'None could have found her without my skills. I traced her scent to the Wantsum. She should, of course, marry me.'

So who do you think Phannetta married?

Sixteen

THAT'S ENOUGH TO BE GOING ON WITH

There was once a little girl and a little boy who lived with their poor old granny in a broken-down old cottage a few miles from Ashford. There was never enough to eat but their Granny had taught them good manners, so when they were given a cabbage leaf or a crust of bread, a taste of cider or a few bones for the soup, they would always say, 'No more thank you, that's enough to be going on with.' People liked them for their fine manners despite their poor clothes. In this way they scraped by.

Not far from the cottage there was a large farm and in it there lived a mean, fat farmer. He had corn ricks, a herd of cows and an apple orchard. He always knew exactly how many apples he had, how much milk the cows had given and he never spilt any grain or wasted it. He never gave anything to anyone, especially the boy or girl but shooed them off his land with curses, reproving them for stealing (which they weren't).

He accused the granny of being a witch (which she wasn't) and threw stones into her garden. He said that she was taking milk from his cows, which was not true, despite the goat giving only a sup of milk each day for the three of them to share. As the children wandered along the road-side with the goat to find

enough grass for her to eat the farmer would rant and rave that all the grass belonged to him (which it didn't).

One winter's day the goat was so hungry that she broke free of her tether and ran into the Little Men Wood, where the grass was lush and thick. The children were scared; no one went into these woods, everyone said they belonged to the Little People. But they ventured slowly in and called out cautiously, 'We are very sorry, we do beg your pardon but our goat ran into your woods and she must be fetched back. We don't mean to trespass.' No reply came from the woodland folk.

As they walked deeper into the trees an amazing sight met their eyes. Everywhere was covered in strawberries, great clusters of the red fruit in heaps as far as they could see. The goat was eating them as fast as she could. The children cried out, 'We're so sorry our goat is eating your strawberries. We can't seem to stop her. May we take a handful to our Grandmother? She is always hungry, as are we.'

Shrill, scratchy voices surrounded them saying, 'Pick and eat as many as you like.' Now this was not as kind as it sounded as these were enchanted strawberries and you could never stop eating them once you had eaten one. The only way to stop was to say 'thank you', which of course the children did after the first few. They even said 'thank you' for the goat, which stopped her eating immediately. They thanked them for the berries that they had picked for granny and took themselves and the goat off to their home.

They must have pleased the Little Men because the goat gave plenty of rich, creamy milk from then on. Amazingly, strawberries grew in the cottage garden all through the year. The berries attracted the attention of the farmer one winter's day as they glowed, juicy red in the snow. He burst through the gate and said, 'Where did you get those strawberries from? You must have stolen them from my fields.' Of course he had no berries in his fields; it was the wrong time of the year.

'No, no,' they replied, 'they came from Little Men Woods.'

'Those woods are mine too,' lied the farmer. Now the Little Men have sensitive ears and they heard the lie and giggled to each other. The farmer popped a strawberry into his mouth, then another and another. In half an hour he had eaten all the berries in the garden and was still raving for more.

'Give me strawberries, I must have more strawberries,' he demanded. They told him that Little Men Woods were full of them and he rushed off to fill his belly. When he reached the woods he didn't ask permission to enter, he marched in and stuffed strawberries into his mouth as fast as he could. He couldn't have said thank you even if he had wanted to (which he didn't), his mouth was too full. All that day and into that night he ate and all the next day too and the day after that. They heard the bang from the cottage and as far as Ashford when he exploded at the weekend; and faintly, the sound of the Little Men laughing.

Seventeen

RED JACKET

There were once three tired men wandering along a lonely path on the Kentish North Downs. They were neither old nor young but you could see in their worn faces that they had seen some interesting times. They wore what was left of their uniforms; torn jackets, rain-washed caps and ragged trousers. They had all been soldiers – good soldiers but now there was no war to fight. The war had finished and all any of them knew about was soldiering. Oh, they could march, fire a gun and fight all day but now nobody would pay them to do it. They discussed this as the road led them deeper into a wood.

'Cobblers; boot and shoe repairs. That's what every town has, cobblers. I'm good with me hands, I could be a cobbler,' said the short man as he stared at his toenail poking though the end of his boot.

'That's the trouble, Harold. Every town already has a cobbler,' explained the ex-soldier with the moustache. 'I shall be a farmer. You never meet a hungry farmer. A good living is to be had on the land. I can see meself now…'

Richard the red-haired man interrupted. 'And I can see you starving Thomas, who will give you land, seed or animals? There are many thousands like us wandering the county of Kent; the same in Essex, Dorset or Wiltshire. Begging, that's what we will do. I'll make a crutch and limp a bit, play the "old soldier" act.'

'No need for an act, you are an old soldier,' grunted the short man.

They stomped along in silence. The road grew narrow, became a path and almost disappeared. The sun set and the trees grew closer together. An owl screeched in triumph as it caught a vole. Things scuttled in the undergrowth. The men decided that they would not reach the town today but that they must make a camp and sleep in the woods. They found a clearing and gathered some fallen timber for a fire.

Things slithered around the men as they settled down for the night. Bats flittered low over their heads. Something howled not very far away. You would think that soldiers would be brave, wouldn't you? Well, they are when they are fighting, but they are no keener on having a spider wriggling down the neck or a snake slithering up the trouser leg than you are. And that had sounded like a wolf, hadn't it? They agreed that one would stay awake for the first three hours and then he would wake the next man to keep watch. After his three hours he, in turn, would wake the last for his 'watch'. Richard the red-headed man said he would guard first. The others settled down and were soon snoring.

Richard sat on a stump and tried not to hear the things rustling in the brambles. His stomach rumbled with hunger as he warmed his hands by the fire. Then he remembered something that would raise his spirits. He felt in his pocket and – yes – there it was. It was half of the iron-hard ration biscuit that had been given to him when he had been discharged from the army two weeks ago. If he sucked it maybe it would soften in his mouth. He took it out of his pocket and started to pick off the dirt and fluff.

From behind a tree appeared a wondrous sight. There was a little man, no bigger than a rabbit, wearing a red jacket and sporting a wide red hat with a red feather in it. He had bright eyes and a big red beard. He looked at the red-headed man's hand then into his eyes. His voice was like pebbles rattling in a wooden bucket.

'Red Jacket likes biscuit. Red Jacket smells biscuit. Gentleman share with Red Jacket?'

Soldiers always share and the red-headed man was still, at heart, a soldier. His knuckles turned white as he attempted to break the biscuit in two but when it did break with a loud crack one half was much bigger than the other. Well, he thought, it'll be hard to eat anyway. He passed the larger of the pieces to Red Jacket.

You wouldn't have thought, watching the little man, that he was eating a small piece of biscuit. He filled his mouth and chewed, smacked his lips and acted as if it were a full meal. After five minutes he wiped his beard, let out a huge belch and patted his stomach.

'Tasty food. Red Jacket grateful. Red Jacket has something for you.'

From under the red jacket came a small green leather purse. Red Jacket handed it to Richard.

The red-headed man took the purse in his hand and tried to look pleased.

'Well,' he said, 'it's a very nice gift I'm sure; beautifully made. A purse for coins, isn't it? The only thing is, well, neither my friends nor I ever have more than a single coin to keep. But thank you very much anyway.'

Red Jacket looked at him with glittery eyes.

'Money in purse; Gold. Always is. Look.'

The red-haired man undid the clasp and shook a gold coin out into his hand. Firelight reflected from the shiny metal. This was the most valuable coin he had ever touched. It was heavy in his palm.

'This is most generous. This will feed and shelter us three for months. Thank you very much.'

'Money still in purse. Look again.'

The purse was tipped again and another gold coin fell out.

'Money always in purse. Always. Forever,' said the red-bearded dwarf.

He was right. Every time the purse was tipped another coin fell out. There was soon a glistening heap of them spilling from Richard's hand onto the grass below.

'Time flies,' grunted Red Jacket, 'your watch over. Must go.' He walked behind a tree and disappeared.

The red-haired man saw that the moon that had been low in the east was now nearly overhead. Three hours must have somehow passed while he was talking to the dwarf. He shook the shoulder of Thomas who awoke with a grunt.

'Thomas! Time for your watch,' whispered the red-haired man, 'Now, keep your eyes open for a little man in a red jacket. I was a little bit generous to him and he was very generous to me. I'll tell you more in the morning.' He wrapped himself in his blanket and settled himself down to sleep.

The man with the moustache sat by the fire and thought about what the other man had said. Little man? Red jacket? Out here in the woods? He must have been dreaming. Thomas shivered despite the fire and worried about the snakes and the wolves. Then he remembered his hip flask. There may be just a taste of apple brandy left, a single drop that would remind him of better times and raise his spirits.

Thomas rummaged in his rucksack and found the flask. He unscrewed the top and tipped it over his open mouth and a single amber drop of brandy quivered hanging on the edge of the neck. It was at that moment that Red Jacket appeared from behind the tree.

'Evenin'. Cold night. Red Jacket likes drink. Red Jacket thirsty.'

The man with the moustache remembered what the red-haired man had said, lowered the flask and passed it to the dwarf. 'Only one drop left, my friend. That's all there is.'

Red Jacket tipped it over his mouth and a great stream of brandy poured out into his mouth, splashing onto his beard and dribbling down his neck. Glug, glug, glug, glug went the flask and the throat; it seemed as if several pints were being swallowed. At last he finished, lowered the flask, wiped his mouth and let out a loud belch. The flask still had a drop of brandy in it.

'Good apple brandy. Red Jacket has gift. Here.'

He held out his grubby hand which seemed to have nothing in it. Thomas looked closely but there was absolutely nothing to see. He had better ask, he thought.

'Very kind I'm sure. What is it?'

Red Jacket reached with his fingers into the palm of his hand and seemed to take something in his finger tips. His other fingers gripped whatever it was and the hands drew apart.

'Red Jacket shows you. Red Jacket here,' he mimed putting a cloak around his head and shoulders, 'Red Jacket gone.'

Red Jacket disappeared. There was no sign of him at all. The man with the moustache found that his mouth had fallen open. 'Where are you?' he cried looking around. Red Jacket's voice came from nowhere.

'Still here. Cloak of Vanishing. Very useful. Hold out hand.'

Red Jacket reappeared. Thomas held out his hand and the dwarf dropped what seemed to be a screwed-up cobweb into the ex-soldier's palm.

'Travelling too. Think of somewhere, cloak will take you.'

The man with the moustache put the screwed-up cobweb carefully into the lining of his hat. Red Jacket said, 'Wake your friend. Much time passed.' He waved a hand and disappeared behind a tree.

Thomas saw that the moon had nearly sunk to the west. 'How could this be?' he thought, 'not five minutes ago it was overhead.' He nudged the short ex-soldier with the toe of his boot. 'Wakey, wakey, Harold, time to rise.' The waking soldier snorted and spluttered. The man with the moustache explained about the little man with the red jacket but the sleepy head was not ready to listen, the head was still full of dreams. Groggily he rose as the other settled himself down.

He shivered in the half-dark of early dawn and wished that he were still asleep. He put his hands in his pockets and discovered the bowl of his old tobacco pipe. Ah, he thought, there may be a shred of tobacco left in there. Enough for just one warming puff. As he put the pipe in his mouth and felt in his pocket for a match Red Jacket walked round the tree. His eyes shone as he looked at the pipe.

'Red Jacket enjoys a puff.'

'I'm sure he does.' said the short man, 'but there is only a tiny speck of 'baccy in here. It would be an insult to offer it to you.'

'Red Jacket small. Speck is enough,' said the little man as he held out his hand.

'There you go, then,' said the soldier passing it over.

The dwarf put the pipe in his mouth, clicked a flame from his thumb and lit the shred of tobacco. Great clouds of smoke billowed from his lips, not just the usual blue-grey but yellows, greens, reds and purples. The clouds formed not into smoke rings but into castles, galleons, flying dragons, galloping horses, silvery mermaids and dancing maidens. There were the flags of all nations and scenes of ancient battles. He blew smoke triangles, knots, pyramids and squares. When he had finished he handed the pipe back and there was still a shred of tobacco in the bottom of the bowl.

'Red Jacket thanks. Here. For you.'

He reached into his jacket to draw out a hollow cow horn with a silver mouthpiece and rim. He handed the horn to the soldier. The man looked at it and said, 'Well, that's very kind of you but I have not a musical bone in my body. I expect I could sell it, though.'

'Magic horn,' said the dwarf, 'not musical. Summons soldiers far and wide; past, present, future. To help you.'

The short soldier thanked him, took the horn and stored it in his shoulder bag.

'Be careful with gifts. Powerful magic. Don't lose 'em,' growled Red Jacket as he vanished behind the tree.

The short soldier was surprised to be blinded by a shaft of low sunlight heralding the dawn. It was time to wake the others. He nudged them with the toe of his boot until they got up.

'Right,' announced Richard the red-haired soldier, 'follow me, lads. I can smell frying bacon and I have gold. I shall buy you the finest breakfast you have ever tasted.'

They showed each other their gifts as they followed the wonderful bacon aroma through the woods and into the town. They ate a huge breakfast of sausages, eggs, bacon and fried bread until lunchtime and then started on lunch, which went on until teatime.

They decided to tell no one about their gifts or Red Jacket, but to use the bottomless purse carefully. Splendid clothes, six fine horses and a stable, a large house and garden; all this spending and still the gold flowed from the purse.

Their large house was right in the centre of
the town, a good address up against the
walls of the palace where the King and
his daughter, Princess Drean, resided.
It was in a good position, convenient
for the shops and the alehouse, but
in the shade for two hours every day.
Casting this very long shadow was
Princess Drean's tower. Built by the
fairy folk at her command it was so
high that the moon scraped the flag
pole at the top as it passed. Princess
Drean had commanded the little
folk to start and then she had gone
shopping and forgotten all about
them so they had just carried on
building, higher and higher. The
servants cursed as they climbed
the stairs for hours to reach the
Princess's room; Princess Drean

had no such problems, she was a sorceress, she could fly.

Not that people, even her father the King, had realised that she
was a sorceress. Her nose was small and pretty, not hooked like
a witch. No red wizard eyes for her; pale blue corneas and long
lashes made men stare at her beauty. Her hair was the colour of
silver and flowed down her back as silky as a waterfall. It didn't
writhe like serpents, which was the latest fashion amongst the
magical society ladies.

So, what of the ex-soldiers? Well, with a fine house, smart
clothes and endless money Richard decided that he could make a
social visit to the princess and maybe pitch his woo. He had heard
that she was rich, lovely and unmarried, why not? He went to the
barber and had his red hair cut and his chin shaved and by golly he
looked smart. He put the magical purse in his pocket, straightened
his braided jacket, brushed the loose hair from his trousers and
marched to the bottom of the Princess's tower.

He told the soldier on guard that he would like to meet the princess and asked if she were at home. The guard saluted (he knew a military man when he saw one) and directed him upstairs. The spiral staircase wound up and up in what seemed to be an endless succession of worn steps. After an hour his knees started to ache. Two hours later his feet hurt, his toes throbbed and he was starting to pass the skeletons of chaps who had tried the climb before and had died of exhaustion. At last he came to a carved bronze door guarded by two bored soldiers. They paid no attention to him so he gave the door a timid knock.

He could hear the low murmur of young female voices. The door swung open and there was an extremely pretty lady in a beautifully embroidered dress covered in pearls. She gestured that he should enter and he bowed deeply and walked in on wobbly legs to discover that the pretty lady was only a maid and that Princess Drean was even lovelier in an even more beautiful dress. He was sat down and given a cup of tea and a biscuit.

The Princess Drean was polite and attentive but now and again she would stifle a half-concealed yawn behind her hand. He told her of the war and being in the army but she gazed out of the window and didn't show much interest until, in a desperate attempt to impress her, he showed her the magical purse. He demonstrated that it held limitless wealth. As the pile of gold coins grew she smiled, gazed at him intently and ordered more tea for them both with a concealed wink to her maid.

The tea arrived and the soldier drank his without tasting it, so amazed was he that the princess should now smile so sweetly and find him so fascinating. Soon the drugged tea and his exhaustion forced his eyes closed and he slept. The princess prised his hand open, took the purse and sent it on a very long piece of string down to the fourth floor of the tower. Pinned to the purse was a note to her seamstress with instructions to make an exact copy of the purse with a gold coin in it to send back up the tower.

When the soldier awoke he apologized to the princess for falling asleep but she was so sweet and gracious about it that he smiled as he left, thinking perhaps that next time he might risk a quick kiss.

Down and down he went until he was at the bottom and soon he was home. He told the others all about the princess and his tea, saying he thought that he might buy her a handsome gift for his next visit. In his room he tipped the first gold coin out of his purse and then tipped it up for the next one. There wasn't a next one. He shook it harder; nothing. He turned it inside out, still nothing.

'Hey, chaps. Come up here. My magical purse has run out of magic. One gold coin and no more; look.'

The other two came in and they tried to get more coins out with spoons and shouting but nothing worked. Thomas asked if he had given the purse to anyone else to hold but the red-haired man said he hadn't.

'I didn't take my eyes off it at all except – ah, yes, I did close my eyes for a moment. It's a long way up that tower and I was exhausted.'

'Then maybe this is not your purse. Shall I use my cloak of travelling and invisibility to look for you?'

'Yes please. Right at the top of the tower is the Princess's room.'

Thomas took the Cloak of Wishing and Invisibility from his hat lining, unfurled it and wished himself into the Princess's tower room. He should have thought about the whole escapade a little harder. When he suddenly appeared in the tower room the ladies were shocked and surprised and let out shrill screams. The guards burst through the door and the man with the moustache, being a soldier himself, realised that he was unarmed and outnumbered. He did what he had been trained to do, retreat to fight another day. He jumped out of the window.

He had no idea how high up he was until he was out. He hadn't climbed those stairs for hours to get there like the red-haired man but had used the magic of the cloak. It was a fine day and he had a superb view across rolling hills and shining lakes, snowy peaks glinting below a few wispy clouds. He could see the sea in the distance one way and a desert in the other. Birds flew in great flocks below him. The ground seemed a long way away, the town below looked like a child's toy. The wind whistled through his moustache.

He wasn't worried. All he had to do was wrap the Cloak of Wishing and Invisibility round himself and wish himself home. He calmly waved to a passing skein of geese then looked for the cloak. It wasn't in his hat. It wasn't in his pocket. He searched quicker and quicker, searching even ridiculous places like his nostrils, his belly button and his ears. It was not there. It had, of course, caught on a nail in the window frame as he had jumped out.

The ground grew closer and he began to believe that he was about to die. 'What should be my last words?' he thought. 'Something brave or noble, I suppose. But I expect it will be "BOTHER" as usual. 'BOTHER!' As it happened he met a great clump of ivy first; he smashed through it in a cloud of leaves and surprised birds and continued on down a little bit slower. Two more clumps, a flagpole, a few swallows' nests and a gargoyle and he was falling as slowly as a man jumping from a stable roof. When he hit the soft mud of the moat it splashed up the tower and ruined all the clean washing hanging outside the second story laundry and the man with the moustache was filthy ... but alive.

'Don't ask,' snarled Thomas when he met the others, 'just don't ask. No, I didn't get your confounded purse and yes, I did lose the Cloak of Wishing and Invisibility. Let's hear no more about it.'

'We still have my present, the horn,' muttered Harold, 'we can still summon help.'

'Go on then,' the man with the moustache said, picking bits of swallow's nest out of his ears, 'but we're up against a princess and a king and all his soldiers. We will need lots of help.'

'Watch this,' said the short soldier putting the horn to his lips. He took a deep breath, blew and a noise like a mouse fart came out; 'Feeep'.

'Very magical,' said Thomas.

They felt it through their feet first. A shaking; the ground quivering as if an earthquake was happening. Then the noise came, a rumble so deep that you felt it in your chest. Then they heard sounds of tracks squeaking, feet stamping, wheels rolling and wings flapping. They all went to the window and looked down into the street below.

It was usually busy but now there were so many people that the street was jammed solid. Crammed amongst the locals were war horses, armoured camels and fighting elephants. They jostled for place with soldiers on bicycles, pilots in ornithopters, generals in tanks and a hairy man with a sharpened rock. There were many thousands of them, all looking up at the three and waiting for orders.

'Magical enough for you?' sneered the short soldier as he leaned out of the window. He took a deep breath and shouted to the military crowd. He knew what to say, it had been said to him countless times by innumerable sergeant-majors over the years.

'ATT-EN-SHUN! Listen to me you 'orrible lot. Behind this house is a castle. Surround the castle with weapons drawn and await orders. And you with the sharpened rock – get your 'air cut!'

They all spread out left and right and surrounded the castle. The street below became busy with people collecting horse droppings, camel dung and elephant poo. 'Waste not want not' was popular, especially back then. The besieging soldiers made an interesting sight; some in shiny armour, some in camouflage, many sporting long beards and some with fascinating tattoos or war paint. They held rocket launchers, swords, rifles, spears and flamethrowers. They wore berets, bronze helmets, knitted tam-o-shanters and shaved heads. On their feet were sandals, shiny boots and flippers.

The King looked out of the castle window at the huge colourful army and worried. What did they want? He summoned his daughter. Being a princess and a teenager she came when she was good and ready.

'My darling, are these friends of yours? They look a little rough as company for a royal like you, don't you think? Look, one of them has sat on my favourite lavender bush. He's bent it all out of shape. Oh, it will never be the same again, never, never.'

Princess Drean calmed him down. She ordered him a nice cup of tea and a biscuit then sat him down with them under a mulberry tree in the central courtyard where he couldn't see the soldiers. She had a feeling about these soldiers; her sorceress's instinct told her that they were here for a purpose; gathered here magically, judging by the huge variety. They were all very different from each other and yet, somehow, all the same. But they had a weakness. They were all soldiers. They were all men.

She went to the dancing ladies dressing room on the sixteenth floor and chose some bits and pieces of their costumes. Her royal gown was taken off and given to a dancer to wear to allow her to pose as the Princess's double for a while. The dancer's costume that the Princess put on was a pair of finger cymbals, some heavy eye make-up and a filigree of lace. Oh yes, and some shoes with very high heels. A wicked smile of crimson lipstick and she was ready. She walked out to dance for the men.

'Tshing tk tshing tshing tshing tshing,' went the cymbals as she writhed like a snake and fluttered her eyelashes at the soldiers. Soon every eye was watching her and the men's mouths were hanging open. Soldiers, whether ancient Greeks or space marines, are always the same; easily distracted by a good-looking lady. While they were watching her a dancing girl, under Princess Drean's instructions, crept into our heroes' house and stole the horn.

As soon as she had taken the horn, the last of Red Jacket's gifts, the house disappeared causing the dancing girl to fall from what had been a bedroom into what was now a chicken coop. The three soldiers found that their fine clothes had become ragged scraps of uniform again. They were just as they had been before they had met Red Jacket; poor, jobless and with nowhere to live. The Princess Drean was soon up in her tower room, gloating over her stolen gifts.

The soldiers took to the road again, blaming each other for their losses. They argued so much that the short soldier, who was getting wrongly blamed for most of their troubles, took the right fork when the road divided while the other two turned left.

Harold soon found himself deep in the woods again. The sun went down and the moon came up so he decided to settle down for the night under a wild apple tree. As he fell asleep he idly chewed on a piece of apple.

When he woke the sun was rising and he couldn't move. He wondered what was wrong. He tried to look to the left and right but his head was stuck. Something was also blocking the view between his eyes. He crossed his eyes in an effort to see what it was. It was his nose. During the night it had grown long; past his chin, down over his chest and between his legs then away into the grass.

He could see glimpses of it as it snaked through the weeds and stinging nettles. He could feel that it went through a bramble bush, in and out of a cold stream and across a road. More stinging nettles led it through a hedge beyond which he could smell cow pats. Across a ploughed field, through a pig sty, a chicken coop, a farm kitchen and beyond to the pleasures of the horse's stables.

He didn't know what to do. Reel it in and coil it around his waist? Find a wheelbarrow and fold it into that? Wind it round his head? Cutting it off would be too painful, he couldn't do that. He lay with his head against the apple tree and hoped that no heavy wagons came along the road. The stinging from the nettles and the prickles of the brambles were quite painful enough already. He breathed through his mouth; the smells were strong and nasty.

The other two had eaten and slept in a local inn and had been told to chop the firewood to pay for their stay. The chopping had warmed them up and they were almost cheerful as they strode along the road. A mile on and they were surprised to see a long pink snake lying across the road in front of them. Thomas gave it an exploratory kick and from the woods nearby came a familiar voice,

'Oh, be dose!'

'That sounds like our short friend Harold,' said the red-haired soldier and they followed the fleshy snake off the road, through a stream, into patches of brambles and nettles and on into a clearing. They found their friend slumped miserably under the apple tree.

'Be dose grew overnide. I can'd move and the neddles are sting-ing it. And the smells are awful.'

The soldier with the moustache pulled out his long bayonet and tested the edge with his thumb. The blood welled up; it was sharp as a razor.

'Now,' he said soothingly, 'this might sting a bit.'

As he spoke Red Jacket strode out from behind the tree. His glittery eyes gazed at the soldiers calmly and he surveyed the length of the nose. He snorted.

'Someone eaten apple from Nosetree. Someone very silly.'

'Bud wad ab I goig to do?' wailed the soldier.

'Eat pear from Nosetree. Easy.'

'Bear?' queried Harold.

'Bear? Where?' shrieked Red Jacket, leaping up into the low branches of the Nosetree.

'He means 'Pear' but his nose is blocked. Do come down, sir,' Thomas said coaxingly.

'There are no bears.'

Red Jacket calmed down a little and dropped from the tree. 'Pear! Other side of Nosetree. Apples one side, pears the other. Apples grow noses and pears shrink 'em. Use the fruit to get your presents back. You will have to use your heads though, not that you've used 'em much so far. Best of luck. Cheerio.'

'Wait a flaming minute,' said the soldier with the moustache, 'hang about. You can talk like anyone now. Why were you so terse when we met before? What were all those short sentences about?'

'Well,' said Red Jacket, 'I'm magical, aren't I? Gotta sound right if you're magical. People expect it.'

'Born magical, were you?' asked the red-header man.

'Nah, I got caught in a nasty spell of Pratchett when I was three. Wave of magic all across Kent; wells changed into towers, ears where your feet ought to be, Nosetrees, terrible stuff. I became Red Jacket there and then and haven't grown an inch since. Two hundred years ago. Been at it ever since. Cheerio.'

This time he did go, leaving the three soldiers to think. The first thing they did was to find a pear from the other side of the tree and feed bits of it to the short man. Gradually his nose shrank to a more suitable size. The three then debated what to do next. They were not the best at thinking; when they had been soldiers thinking had been very much discouraged. Hear an order and unthinkingly obey it; that was the best way.

However, a few hours later a man in a straw hat was carrying a basket of apples and crying his wares at the base of Princess Drean's tower. The hair under the hat was, of course, red.

'Apples; get your loverely apples. Finest Kent grown. Fit for a princess. Red and shiny. Loverely apples.'

His voice carried up the tower as it was meant to. Soon Princess Drean's head was sticking out of the window high above the clouds. Her voice came down faintly, 'I'm a princess. I want your apples. Come up here with them.'

'Sorry darlin,' can't leave me pitch or some other trader will get it. Anyway, these are for a royal princess. Too good for just anyone.'

'I am a royal princess! I will lower a basket with a pretty gold coin in it down to you and you fill the basket with apples.'

Down came the basket with a familiar-looking gold coin in it and up went the apples. Being a greedy girl Princess Drean stuffed two in her mouth at once. Her nose shot forwards and jammed against the wall next to the window before escaping into the fresh air. Down the tower it went, into the moat and out into the town. There it was squashed by wheels, stamped on by feet and smeared with jam in the bakers before it snaked its way into the countryside.

Because she was a sorceress her nose grew twice as fast as anyone else. Down the Folkestone cliffs went her nose, under the Dover Straits all the way through Flanders across the Holy Roman Empire and on over the frozen Alps where it got very cold. On it went through some very smelly places; Kiev, Volhynia, and Pereyaslavl. It grew even quicker as it crossed from Russia to Alaska. It rushed through Canada and on across the Atlantic Ocean reaching Connaught then Leinster and finally Gwynedd (who had little idea that they would later become Ireland and Wales), until it came back through the window of Princess Drean's Kentish tower room where it poked the Princess in the back of the head.

The Nosetree apples contained strong, old fashioned magic that young sorceresses didn't bother to study. There was nothing she could do. It was horribly embarrassing to be stuck in your room, by your own nose. It wasn't the food; she was used to being fed; she was a princess after all. But she preferred to go to the toilet rather than the toilet being brought to her. There were also nasty sponge-baths and the sensation that camels were nibbling at her nostrils halfway round the world. A girl can't cope with all this. Something must be done, but what?

The next morning a voice wafted gently up the tower and a serving girl leaned out of the window to listen.

'Hear ye, hear ye. I am the famous Doctor Proboscis. Well known in England, Europe and Asia for curing headaches, sweetening smelly feet and nose reduction!'

Had the serving girl been down where he was she could have seen that the Doctor, despite his tall black hat and silvery whiskers, looked suspiciously like the man who had suddenly appeared in the tower room a couple of days before. She relayed the news about the Doctor to Princess Drean. The Princess did have a bit of a headache and she thought her feet may have been a bit smelly but if he could reduce the size of her nose that would be wonderful. She sent the serving girl down to ask him to come up.

By the time the serving girl had gone all the way down and the 'Doctor' had climbed all the way up it was nearly tea-time. The 'Doctor' explained that the medicine for nose reduction only worked with honest people and asked the princess if she had ever stolen anything. She would have shaken her head if she could, but she couldn't so she just said, 'Doh, I've never sdolen anthig.' So he took the two bottles of fruit juice out of his bag and gave her a teaspoon of the apple juice. Her nose shot over her shoulder and out of the opposite window.

'By dose is growig again,' she wailed.

'Perhaps you have not been entirely honest,' suggested the 'Doctor'.

'I might have taken just one tiny magical cow-horn,' she admitted.

The 'Doctor' gave her a hard stare. 'Perhaps if you give the horn to me the medicine will work,' he suggested.

The serving girl was sent to fetch the horn and it was given to the 'Doctor' to 'look after'. He gave her a sip of the pear juice. Her nose shrank out of the back window of the tower and vanished over the horizon.

'Wad aboud a bid more,' questioned the Princess, 'I can sdill smell elephands.'

'Anything else you have taken?'

'Odly a tiny magic cload,' whimpered Princess Drean, 'bud I foud it, I didn't steal it.'

'Let's have it,' demanded the 'Doctor', 'unless you like the smell of elephants?'

The serving girl found the cloak and gave it to the 'Doctor'. He put it carefully away in his 'medicine bag' and gave the Princess another sip of the pear juice, saying 'We must be careful not to overdose; you will need some nose left, if only to keep your eyes apart. Now, was there anything more that you should be returning?'

Princess Drean was frightened by the idea of not having any nose at all so she admitted to the copied purse trick. The purse was returned and the pear juice brought her nose down to a pretty little nub.

The Princess was a reformed character from then on and became a famous queen. The three soldiers settled down in Kent and became prosperous fathers and Grandfathers. In fact, just about every Tom, Dick and Harry born in Kent since then claims them as their ancestors.

Eighteen
THE BITER BIT

A man was cruelly murdered by his wife. Cruelly, because his sins as a husband were few; his Jane had enough to eat and was well dressed for a fishmonger's wife living between Love Lane and Malt Mews in Rochester. This was a poor area on the hill above the river Medway. After the wedding she had quickly got used to his pervasive smell of fish although she often wished that he caught the fish rather than sold them; at least fish from the sea was always fresh. No, his sins were small; sucking his teeth noisily, loud persistent snoring and farts both musical and pungent. Over sixteen years these things can easily erode a marriage and one day a sailor with a twinkle in his eye tipped the balance. The fishmonger had to go.

Their plan was to dispose of the body from Rochester Bridge on the outgoing tide into the Medway where the currents would wash him into the Thames Estuary and thence out into the English Channel. Now this was a very old bridge; parts of it were Roman and a low broken stone balustrade was the only thing that kept people safe from falling into the strong tidal-rips that scoured the Medway twice a day. There was an old story of a troubadour known as 'Harpur a Roucestre', who had been blown off the bridge in a gale, but he had played his harp so well and prayed to the Virgin Mary so fervently as he was swept along by the torrent that he had been cast up safely ashore. Nothing like that would save this man.

It was late at night and the skies were moonless and starless. The River Medway roared and grumbled between the stone arches. Not only was the tide going out but there had been heavy storms upstream that day in Headcorn and Tonbridge. The wife had seen the tumbling water when she had gone to the market, now it was even faster. 'The murder should be done tonight,' she had thought, 'the body will travel far in this torrent.'

The murder itself had been easy; the husband always dozed after his heavy supper. He sat in his chair in front of the fire, his head tipped forward and a sonorous snore vibrating the ornaments on the mantelpiece. The snoring stopped abruptly when she raised her arms high and smashed the heavy flat-iron down onto his head. The solid metal lump made a sucking sound as she pulled it from his broken skull; her gorge rose but she swallowed and kept her thoughts on her lover who would arrive soon to help. She pulled the corpse out to the gutting shed behind the cottage, sewed his fat body into an old hessian sack and when her lover arrived they hauled the heavy carcase onto his back and the lovers took him to Rochester Bridge.

Few people were about that night, they met no one on the way. As they passed the Rochester Cathedral Jane had a pang of conscience; you cannot attend the church all your life without learning what guilt feels like. Down the hill and past the Rochester Castle they trudged but as Jane walked behind her lover and the sack she received a terrible shock. What little light there was revealed her husband's hand hanging from the bundle; a dead hand that seemed to be gesturing 'follow me' as it flopped back and forth with each pace. 'If someone sees that we are done for,' she thought, and called to her sailor to stop. As he waited in a deep shadow she found a large needle and some button thread to fasten the hand back in.

'We ought to put some stones in to weigh the corpse down; just tack it until we reach the bridge,' suggested her sailor lover, 'there will be plenty of loose rock on the parapet.'

She gathered up the rough hessian and put some strong stitches through it as her lover urged her to hurry; the body was heavy, he said.

Soon they were on the bridge and the rushing water below seemed to invite them to do the terrible deed. He backed up to the parapet and rested the body on it. She undid the stitches holding the hand safely concealed and pushed stone after stone into the sack then sewed it up good and tight. Those long, strong stitches will last him all the way to France, she thought.

The lover eased back to tip the corpse into a watery grave. She leaned back too. Jane imagined that he was overbalancing and grasped his lapels. Further back he went until his feet had left the roadway, Jane was screaming as quietly as she could that he must release the corpse. 'The body will fall now, for God's sake let go!' she wailed.

But he had already let go. The reason that he was being dragged into the cold water were the many strong stitches that she had put through the sack that had also gone right through the sailor's clothes. He was sewn to the corpse and he could not unbutton his jacket before the weight of the dead body hauled him out of her hands. He had fallen with a loud splash into the clammy depths. Neither body was ever found and the wife – well, the wife went quietly mad.

Nineteen

THE PICKPOCKETS

A couple of miles north of Canterbury there is a village called Sturry. Once no more than a ford across the River Stour it had, by William and Mary's reign, a church, a couple of watermills, several shops, two pubs and many houses. In one of those houses lived a man and his wife; she was a seamstress and he was a tailor.

Now they loved each other well and when she became pregnant they had great hopes for the offspring. They had heard of a monk, Gregor Mendel, who had written about something called 'acquired characteristics'. Hair colour, build, even cleverness could be handed down to an infant from both mother and father. If the skills of both the parents, nimble fingers and their sharp eyes, came forth in the child they thought what a wonderful needle worker that boy or girl would be.

The baby boy was born and he did have the keen eyes and the clever fingers of his parents. However, he never showed any desire to cut or sew cloth. Young Henry's skills still used the parents virtues but in a very different way. The eyes saw opportunities; the fingers carried them out. At school other children 'lost' things when he was around; pencils, money and sweets vanished from satchels and pockets. But he was never caught stealing; he was too clever for that.

By the age of fourteen he was walking to Canterbury several times a week and refining his thieving skills. So many visitors to the cathedral city had their eyes on the high spires and new sights that it was easy to take their purses, gold watches or wallets. Again, he was never even suspected of robbery.

Henry's ambition grew year by year. The horse-drawn coaches took him to all the crowded, busy markets around; Maidstone, Ashford and Sandwich yielded heavy purses. Visitors to Herne Bay, Whitstable, Ramsgate and Folkstone were just as profitable. Yet his ambition grew more. There was a city where, it was said, the very pavements were made of gold; London.

One morning he caught a lift on a fruit cart from Canterbury to Covent Garden in the centre of the great city. As he entered the metropolis he marvelled at the business and wealth of the trade along the road, the fine carriages and the noble horse riders; opportunities beyond bounds. Here he would become the man-about town, a young blood. Here lay his fortune.

As he backed down the steps of the cart on arrival his pocket was picked. It was done so cleverly that he hardly felt it, but feel it he did; his wallet was gone. He looked carefully at the people around the coach. The farmer, a couple of old men with brooms, some children, a young pretty flower seller ... Ah!

He watched the girl with the flowers. She was pressing her bosom against a gentleman's arm and asking, 'Excuse me, kind sir, could you tell me the way to Whitechapel?'

The man blushed and stuttered, 'Oh! I say. Steady m'dear; Whitechapel? Yes. I think if you go straight down there you can't miss it. You're a bold young gel, aintcha?'

But she was already on her way. He lost his fob watch, his signet ring, his gold fountain pen and his wallet. He didn't notice anything amiss, cheerily waving goodbye as she swayed down the road. She was a brilliant thief so Henry followed her at a distance all that morning and admired her skills.

She took a purse in Drury Lane, a cane and a briefcase in Berwick Street and all the takings of an apple barrow in Covent Garden. He saw her use the side passage to the back of St Paul's Church. As he watched from a distance she lifted a commemorative stone and hid her loot under it. Then, innocent as the spring, she skipped

to a coffee shop and sat at a quiet table. Henry went in and took the seat opposite her; he looked her into her hazel eyes and said, 'Today you stole a fruit cart passenger's wallet with the initials 'H.E.B.' in gold on the inside flap. It contained four gold guineas and three florins.'

She gazed back into his eyes with a smile on her charming lips. 'Sir, if you think that why not call the police? But I am innocent of theft; I have no wallet. Search me if you please.' She opened her cloak to show a thin muslin dress and demonstrated that there was nothing to hide and, besides which, nowhere much to hide it.

'No need for the police,' said Henry, 'besides, they would find nothing unless they searched beneath Lord Arbuthnott's tomb behind St Paul's Church.'

Her healthy complexion turned pale. 'Are you a detective, sir, to know these things? Oh what am I going to do? My poor mother dies of consumption, sir, and needs my constant care.' Tears welled from her eyes.

Henry smiled. 'No need for your tears or my sympathy for your mother. Nor do we need the police. You see, I am a pickpocket, like you. I think we should work together as a team. One to distract and one to take; always someone to pass the item to, leaving the taker 'clean'. We could make a fortune in this rich city of yours.'

'I do well by myself, thank you very much. I think you should take from your patch and I shall take from mine.'

'That is all very well, for now, but do think carefully. If I could catch you, so could the law. Moreover, mine were not the only eyes following your progress today. I noticed an old woman marking your path – perhaps a pickpocket gang guarding their patch. Don't worry; you lost her when you doubled back in Berwick Street. But you may not have much longer in your present career.'

Her tears stopped like a tap being turned off. She smiled and said, 'My name is Rosie and if I ever were to ever share my trade with another – you are just the one I would choose. I can see the truth of what you have said. Come, we have one little visit to make then you must meet my mother.'

They returned to the graveyard behind the church and recovered her day's haul including his wallet, which she returned to him. Her arm linked with his quite naturally as they crossed the Thames and by the time they reached her house they were very good friends. Her jolly mother made them a fine meal before they joined the theatre-going crowds in the West End and began the evening's work. Their supper table that night was covered in bracelets, watches, rings, purses and even a set of gold teeth.

The fences paid them less than half the shop value of the jewellery and watches but their wealth grew quickly. Within a year they had bought a small house in the East End. They commissioned special brass plaques for them to put up in busy areas; each one stamped with the words:

BE ALERT – PICKPOCKETS ARE KNOWN TO OPERATE
IN THIS VICINITY
Check your purse or wallet now!

Of course, all they had to do was be nearby to see where people patted their pockets or looked in their baskets to make their work so much easier. Eventually they bought a fine house in Piccadilly and another out in the Croydon countryside with a grand carriage and horses to take them between.

A year later Henry and Rosie were married in great style; the eating and dancing lasted for three days. They honeymooned on the Isle of Wight and it was not long before she told him that a baby was on the way. He was overjoyed, even more than Rosie was and she asked him if he was particularly fond of babies. 'No, not exactly,' he said, 'but this one could be very special.' And he explained what his mother told him of the monk Gregor Mendel's theories. If Mendel was correct then this child could grow up be the best pickpocket in England, perhaps Europe, maybe the world.

They carried on with their trade together for a few months but confinement was the fashion in those days. This meant bed rest for the expectant lady after the twentieth week, with the best food, nourishing drinks and a daily massage around the belly with oils to ease the birth. After all, this could be a very valuable child and infant death was commonplace.

Henry continued their trade by himself for a while but anxiety for the child made him a regular visitor to his wife's bedside. However, when the labour started he was hustled from the room by the midwife. 'No place for a man,' she said, 'besides, the baby has turned and I must turn it back. No place for a man at all.' The last thing he saw before being pushed into the hall were the fingers of the midwife dipping into a jar of oil.

He could faintly hear the cries of his dear Rosie and the voices of the doctor and the midwife through the door. 'Easy, my dear,' and 'more light here.' Then 'I can feel the cord, it's wrapped around the neck; there, it's free and the child has turned.' then 'Here it comes.

He's a boy!' Then followed by a piercing scream and a baby's first wail. Henry couldn't stop himself bursting through the door.

Rosie was crying with relief and joy as the now silent child was put into her arms. Henry looked with admiration at his infant's narrow pickpocket's fingers protruding from the blanket. The baby looked back at him with sharp, observant eyes. Henry reached down and lifted the blanket to see more. The baby's right arm was tight against the tiny chest, the hand clenched into a hard fist. Henry tried to pull it away but the child resisted and screamed. Henry let it go to the disapproving glares of the midwife and Rosie.

'I simply wanted to see his fingers,' whispered Henry, with a warning look to Rosie.

The midwife had no idea that this opulent house was the result of crime. She took the distressed child and comforted him. 'Could you open his hand?' asked Henry. The midwife gently pulled the tiny fist but the baby wailed again. No one could take the arm away from the chest or open the hand. The doctor tried with no success. Rosie waited until he was asleep and tried but he woke with a reproachful look and resisted. They tried warming it up with hot towels and cooling it down with ice. No ointments or unguents made any difference and none of the surgeons or doctors in London could help.

No experts in Bristol or Birmingham, Cambridge or Oxford had any effect either. It was a crusty old Scottish surgeon in Edinburgh, Dr. James Braid, who made a profound observation.

'Can ye not see,' he growled, 'that the bairn's arm is mighty strrong. Therre is nothing feeble aboot that arm. Noo, I ken the problem is in his wee heed.'

Rosie and Henry looked at one another. 'Heed?' Was he speaking English? The Scotsman continued.

'Therre is a man in Austria, in Vienna, a Dr. Frrranz Mesmer, who has discovered something called 'Animal Magnetism' or 'Hypnotism'. Apparently it helps us to ken what is going on inside the skull, in the brrrain. And all done without surgery so dinna worry yoursen aboot that. Write to Dr Mesmer, mention the name of Brrraid, and ask him to see ye.'

Neither Henry nor Rosie had spent much time at school learning to write so they dictated a letter to one of the servants. Three weeks later a letter arrived from Vienna inviting all three to Dr Mesmer's consulting room. By train to Dover, ferry to France then to Brussels by train and on to Frankfurt, Nuremberg and Linz by coach. They were weary and dirty by the time they reached Vienna and found at last the consulting rooms of Dr Franz Mesmer.

The infant was sat on the leather-covered desk in front of Dr Mesmer. The surgeon stared hard into the child's eyes and the child stared hard back. The doctor removed his Swiss pocket watch from his waistcoat pocket and dangled it in front of baby's eyes, left and right, left and right. The gold watch glittered with tiny jewels. The child's eyes never left the watch, following it back and forth, back and forth.

'You are feeling sleepy, liddle one, your eyelids are soo heavy that you must fall asleep, asleep.' Dr. Mesmer's voice was low and hypnotic, but the baby was highly alert.

'Sleep, liddle one, sleep.'

Then it happened. The tiny fist, curled shut since before he was born, shot forward and opened to grab the watch. The midwife's gold wedding ring, the one that the baby had stolen before his birth, fell to the floor. He was, at the very least, the youngest ever pickpocket in the world.

Twenty

MRS VEAL VISITS

Mary Veal was not married. She kept the Custom House in Dover for her brother and she was a pious, uncomplaining lady of some thirty years. Yet she had much to complain about. Her brother was a dull, sober man; dour and silent. Her father did not allow any money to her or her brother so they scraped by on a custom man's salary, usually only enough to support a single body. Mary Veal was often hungry for both food and company.

Her health was not good either. For many years she had suffered from occasional fits; in the middle of a conversation there would be a sudden pause, her face would become expressionless, her eyes distracted and maybe an inappropriate word would escape from her innocent lips. She would then continue after a moment or two as if nothing untoward had happened.

None of this disturbed her friend since childhood, Mrs Margaret Bargrave. The two ladies had much in common; they were of a similar age, they were both devout Christians and were very interested in spiritualism and what happens to a person after death. Both had suffered fathers who were not generous although Mrs Bargrave had enough allowance to enable her to be helpful to Mary Veal. They would often have tea together and discuss the books they had read about the afterlife; Drelincourt's, *Christians Defense against the Fears of Death,* was a favourite volume with which to exercise their minds. It seemed from this that the more

suffering that they endured in
this life the greater reward they
would receive in the next.

On Saturday, 8 September
1705, Mrs Bargrave had not
seen Mary Veal for over two
years. They had drifted apart
since the Custom House had
become part of Mary Veal's
duties and, besides which,
Mrs Bargrave had a husband
who was an abusive drunk.
He gambled and visited
prostitutes and had so
scandalised the locals that
he had been driven out of
Dover to Canterbury for
his outrageous behaviour
over a year ago. So
Mrs Bargrave was surprised when she opened the door of her
Canterbury house to find a figure in a riding habit; Mary Veal.

Mrs Bargrave smiled and cried, 'It is such a long time since
last we met,' and leaned forewords to kiss her but Mary Veal
leaned back and covered her eyes with her hand saying, 'I am not
well, Mrs Bargrave.' The church bell tolled twelve deep chimes.
Mrs Bargrave showed Mary into her living room and sat her down.

They chatted about their lives and about their situations.
They discussed, as usual, the afterlife and whether ghosts were lost
souls or visitors from hell. Mary Veal uncharacteristically refused
tea or cake but soon came to the reason for her visit. She had, she
said, to start a long voyage on the next Monday and there was some
business that she hadn't found time to do. Would Mrs Bargrave be
so kind as to do some errands for her?

Mary Veal's mother had died last year and had been buried in
Dover but unfortunately, at the time, there had been not enough
money for a gravestone. Now, though, there was enough money

but no time to arrange the work with a stonemason before she went away. Would Mrs Bargrave be so kind as to choose a reliable workman and give him the details of the inscription that was required? Mary Veal took a piece of paper from her handbag and handed it to Mrs Bargrave. There were some words written in Mary's distinctive italic scrawl:

HERE LYES THE BODY OF SUSANNE MARIA VEAL CITIZEN
AND MARCHANT SEAMSTRESS OF DOVER WHO WAS BORNE
AND DYED IN THIS PARISH AFTER SHE HAD LIVED IN THE FEARE OF GOD THREE SCORE & FOURTEENE YEARES
AS BY HER DEEDS OF PIETY AND CHARITY MAY APPEARE
SHE WAS BURIED THE 20TH OF AUGUST 1704 STILO ANGLIAE
IAM SEPVLTVS TANDEM RESVRGAM
ALSO
THE BODY OF MARY VEAL HER DAUGHTER

Mrs Bargrave was surprised that she was preparing for her grave at such a young age. She protested as much to Mary but her words were ignored and a vacant look passed over Mary Veal's features. Mrs Bargrave promised to arrange for the gravestone and accepted some money to cover the expenses. Mary made a further request.

'There is also a matter of the distribution of a few of my affects. Would you write to my brother, Mr Veal, and ask him to distribute my few valuables as described in this note?'

This correspondence was to include details of various personal bequests to be distributed among Mary's friends and relatives in the event of her death. Margaret was again shocked and asked assurance of Mary's health but again the visitor looked distracted and pale. After a couple of hours Mary said that she had other errands to run in Canterbury and made her farewell of Mrs Bargrave.

Mrs Margaret Bargrave was unwell the next day but when she ventured out into the Canterbury streets on the Monday an acquaintance asked her if she had heard the news from Dover – Mary Veal had been taken ill on the preceding Friday and had sadly died. Mrs Bargrave dismissed the news as nonsense, saying that she had been visited by Mary Veal on the Saturday, the day after her supposed death. Further investigations in Dover found that the news was true, Mary Veal had been taken with one of her fainting fits on the Friday morning and after three hours in her bed she had died.

Mrs Bargrave couldn't keep this news to herself and it soon became a celebrated proof of life after death. Daniel Defoe took up the story and included it in his English translation of Drelincourt's, *Christians Defense against the Fears of Death*. Soon the story was receiving royal interest from Queen Anne and a psychical society for the investigation of such phenomena was founded on the strength of it.

Twenty-one

THE MAN WHO COULD UNDERSTAND ANIMALS

Sam the shepherd was sitting on a hot summer hillside watching his flock of sheep. Well, it wasn't really his flock; they belonged to Farmer Gittens who hired him but Sam knew them all better than anyone else did. They were Romney sheep; strong with broad backs and all one big family; three Grandmother ewes, forty-one mothers and aunts and this year over 120 lambs. The ewes nibbled the bleached grass in the sunshine and the lambs leapt as if surprised by everything. By Sam's side sat the two shepherd dogs that were also not his, yet he felt that only he could really understand their yelps and growls. Only he knew where to scratch the spot between their shoulder blades where a paw couldn't reach.

The chalky hillside belonged to the farmer too. Sibertswold was the village at the bottom of the hill; from where Sam stood, smoke and cooking fragrances drifted up from a few chimneys as housewives cooked evening meals. But there was also smoke just beyond the flock; something, maybe a spark from one of those fires, had landed on the sun-dried grass. Sam thought, 'Wherever it came from, the grass shouldn't burn; besides which

it may harm the silly sheep.' Sam picked up
his shepherds crook and with a 'stay' word
to the dogs he walked down the hill to the
smouldering patch.

It was a circle of flames that surrounded
something alive that writhed in the heat. Sam
blinked his eyes in the smoke and looked
closer. There on the scorched grass was a
snake with scales that glittered like jewels
of blue, green and scarlet. It knotted and
shrank from the fire. Now, Sam was a man
who had cared for animals all his life – and a
snake was animal after all. He could no
more let the snake suffer than he could
leave a ewe struggling upside-down in a
ditch or ignore a lamb tangled in the bramble
thorns. He stretched out his arm and lowered his shepherds
crook to lift the snake out and over the flames. The serpent had
a better idea. It coiled around the crook and slithered upwards.
When it reached Sam's wrist it kept going up his arm to his elbow,
on to his shoulder and it coiled quite tightly round his neck.

Sam resisted the temptation to grab and pull at the creature.
It could be poisonous; it may bite him despite his kindness.
Animals can do anything when they are frightened. The snake's
head floated a couple of inches in front of Sams' face. It did not
look at all frightened. The unblinking reptilian eyes fixed upon
his; the forked tongue flickered. The snake spoke, 'Ssso. You sssave
sssnakesss from fire. Sssomething that mussst be repaid. I am the
Princsse of Sssnakes. My father will reward you.'

Sam didn't often speak to anyone, certainly not snakes. He
stuttered a reply, 'I-I ask f-for no reward. Only that you do not b-bite
me or my dogs or sheep. Or t-tighten your grip on m-my neck.'

'My father, the King of Sssnakesss, has not seen a human in
many a long year. Sscertainly not one as generous sssspirited as you.
You mussst meet him. Walk me to the top of the hill.' The pressure
on Sam's neck increased slightly.

Sam couldn't see any way of not doing as he was asked. The top of the hill was one great bald boulder of green-grey chalk surrounded by a dense crown of nettles and brambles. Many a lamb had been caught in them, so Sam had walked around this stone time and again over the years. Never had Sam seen the great split in the rock that he walked into now.

'Ssstop,' hissed the snake.

Sam's eyes adjusted to the darkness of the cleft. Doors at the far end, 12ft high, blocked the way. Doors that looked like intricate tapestries, with fragments of rich colour and patterns that rippled as if blown by a breeze – yet the air was still. Then at a hiss from the prince the doors, which were made of knotted snakes, dropped to the ground and slithered out past Sam's feet. Sam took a deep breath and tried to be calm.

'Prosssceed.'

The cave inside the top of the hill was dimly lit but Sam could make out a raised dais supporting a carved wooden throne. On an embroidered cushion coiled the King of Snakes. His scales were loose and mottled with age – but his eyes were sparkling and wise. The Prince of Snakes whispered into Sam's ear, 'My father will offer you jewelsss; refusse them. He will try to give you money or land; refusse them too. Asssk for the ability to undersssstand animalssss. He musssst give it to you, it isss your right.'

Sam thought, 'That would be very useful,' so he simply said, 'Thank you,' and walked forward to the throne. The King stared at Sam without any expression. His voice was low and scratchy, 'What ith your name, human?'

'Sam is what they call me, sir.'

'Tham. A thplendid name. And a thplendid deed, to have thaved my thonth life. Thomething that thnakes will thpeak of to their anthessthors. What will be your reward? Gold? Thilver?'

'That's a very kind offer, thir – I mean sir. But wealth is not for me; I have seen men destroyed by too much money.'

'Fieldth, then, grath for your own lambth. Potheth your own flock and be your own mathter with your own houth.'

'Er – no thank you.'

'Jewelth; rubieth, diamondth or pearlth?'

'I believe you can make me able to understand the language of animals, sir. Now that is a gift I would like.'

'Tho. A powerful and dangerouth gift ith your requetht. Do you underthtand that if you tell anyone of your ability that your head will burtht into a thousand pietheth?'

'Sir, there are times when I speak to no one but the sheep or the dogs for months. The chances of letting the secret slip out are tiny.'

The King of Snakes looked at him coldly for a moment. 'Come to me, Tham.'

Sam walked up to the King of Snake's throne and stood before it.

'Come clother,' said the King.

Sam took another pace forward. Now the snakes head was an inch from Sam's nose. The snake's mouth opened, his split tongue slithered out. It vibrated and a purple vapour poured into Sam's face. It was like cedar smoke and pepper; incense and gunpowder. Sam felt as if his lungs would burst. When it cleared he blinked for a moment or two, he gave a little cough and thanked the King of the Snakes for his gift. He bowed and the Prince of Snakes indicated that he should leave.

When he was outside the full impact of the gift hit him. The air was full of bird conversations; sparrows argued, robins shouted 'all this is mine' at the tops of their voices and seagulls spoke of smelly fish and distant harbours. The worms in the earth muttered, 'burrow and dig, burrow and dig, squirt it out the back' monotonously and the butterflies in the air hummed happily as they flew. The sheepdogs were there; one asleep and the other watching the flock. The sleeping one muttered, 'Smy bone you stupid rat,' in her sleep and her son said, 'Only a dream, mother,' in a bored growl.

The sheep were a hum of silly conversations; the lambs simply repeating 'Bouncy, bouncy, bouncy, BOUNCY' or 'Maa. Mum? Mummy? Where are you? Where am I? MAA!' and the older sheep saying things like 'Haven't felt right since the shearing. Awful cut, can't do a thing with it,' and 'Get that Daisy; one rosette at the County Show, three lambs and she thinks she's queen of the flock.

I knew her when she was a tatty little thing larking on and off the dung heap.'

Now that Sam could overhear the animals his work was easier; tender paws and stomachs were treated, no animal went hungry or thirsty. He discovered that cats can be terribly rude, mice amazingly brave and horses unsurprisingly vain. One autumn day he was sitting eating some bread and cheese with his back against a dead tree on the hillside. There was a fluttering noise above his head as two rooks landed on a withered branch. An avian conversation could be overheard.

'Kraaah. Now this is a tree with a bit of history, my lad. Kraaah.' The great split in the oak and the scorch marks made it obvious to Sam that it had been struck by lightning sometime in the distant past. Was that the history that the crow mentioned? The raven continued.

'Kraaah. How many summers you had? D'you remembers me tellin' you of the great robbery? Kraaah. That was a laugh all right.'

'Kreeh. Two and a half summers, dad. What's a rubbery? Kreeh.'

'Kraaah. Robbery not rubbery, you fluffy twit. Robbery is when fings are taken, stolen like. Rubbery is what a cowhide what's bin in the stream for few days is like. Kraaah.'

'Kreeh. Robbery, then. Is robbery a laugh?'

'Kraaah. Not for the fief. He stole all their old treasure from the Mansion house. When they caught him they hung him right here, from this branch right over the treasure he had buried below these here roots. Kraaah. He were very annoyed, but not for long.'

Sam cocked his ear and listened carefully. 'How long do rooks live?' he wondered. He remembered the priest telling him of a Greek man who had heard that rooks lived for 200 years and had decided to keep one to see if it was true. This shattered oak had been like this since he was a boy running the streets of Sibertswold. He had never heard of a hanging here.

'Did you have 'is eyes, dad, did you, was they nice?'

'Kraaah. I'll fank you to remember to caw when you speak to me, my lad! Kraaah!'

'Kreah. Sorry dad. But did you, did you?'

'Nah, all before my time. Kraaah. I fink me great great-grandfather may have had one though. It was 'im what told me the story.'

'Kreeh. Who had the treasure, ven?'

'Kraaah. Nobody. Still down there. C'mon, there's a calf been dead three days over Coldred. Race you there. Kraaaaaaah!'

The rooks flapped away into the blue. Sam thought back to what he had said to the King of Snakes; that he had seen men ruined by wealth. Besides which, this tree and the hillside belonged to Farmer Gittens. Anything on Farmer Gittens' land was, in Farmer Gittens' opinion, his to keep; Sam remembered the neighbour's wandering chickens. They never went back. He had better tell the farmer tomorrow.

Farmer Gittens had eyebrows that shot up and down as he listened or spoke. As he was mostly bald the constant raising of the eyebrows usually eased his hat higher and higher until it fell off the back of his head. When Sam arrived after breakfast and told him that there had been a conversation overheard from a pair of 'visiting strangers' about treasure buried beneath his old dead tree his eyebrows leapt up under his hat and weren't seen for an hour. A short time later the two of them were on their way to the tree with mattocks, saws and spades.

After an hour of digging and sawing through old roots, (by Sam, of course), the remains of an iron-bound wooden chest was unearthed. The treasure was old, very old. The gold and silver coins showed profiles of long dead kings and queens, the words beneath them named Saxon rulers; Coenwolf was the only readable one. There were gold dishes and cups, pieces of armour glistening with an inlay of precious metals, gold torcs and bracelets, rubies and diamonds. Farmer Gittens' hat flew right off. In all, more wealth than three ordinary men could spend in a lifetime. Farmer Gittens was a fair man; Sam had discovered it so he gave a third of it all to Sam.

Well, for three days Sam kept the treasure in the sack he had carried it home in. Now and then he would open the sack to make sure it was not all a dream but on the third day he took a golden spoon out and rubbed it with a cloth. It gleamed, which reminded

Sam of the riches seen in the jeweller's shop in Dover. Sam paid the shop a visit. In exchange for a golden spoon he had a pocket full of coins.

The first item he bought was a good pair of boots. Then he paid a rare visit to the barber for a haircut and shave. This was followed by a large meal at the inn; lobster, roast beef and a honey tart. A fine waistcoat and a gentleman's hat were tried and rejected as too smart, too comfortable and not hardwearing enough. As the days and weeks passed there were more visits to the jeweller's shop and he slowly became used to the notion that he had lots and lots of money.

After a season had gone by Sam had bought the cottage that he lived in, had had a well dug, bought the flock of sheep and the dogs from Farmer Gittens and had become his own master and a smart man about the village. For the people of Sibertswold it was as if a handsome stranger had come to live amongst them; for the first time Sam became a social animal; seen at the market, in the church and even in the pub. It was at the market that the widow, Penny Groat, first caught sight of him.

Now Widow Groat had been living in the village for ten years or more. Some said that her husband had been lost at sea, for if she ever did mention him it was as 'The Captain'. Others gossiped about him as a soldier killed in battle. Whichever, he must have had a pension which gave Widow Groat enough to live on comfortably. She gave Sam a nice smile over the cheese stall one warm Wednesday morning and it all went on from there.

They had tea together in Deal, shrimps on the harbour wall in Ramsgate and arm-in-arm they went to the harvest supper in the great tithe barn where they danced until midnight. They walked, hand-in-hand, all the way to Barfrestone Church to wonder at the ancient carvings around the door. Penny Groat rode a fine half-Arab stallion so Sam bought a mare from a farmer at Barham and learned to ride it. Her legs were strong and her back was broad, in contrast to the slender half-Arab. They rode out together and became a familiar, if odd, sight; he, narrow and fit on his stout mare and she, large and wobbly, perched on her slender noble beast. It was only two summers after that they had met that they were married.

Marriage was a bit of a shock to Sam; for one thing he had never seen a woman's bare legs before. He had no idea how long it could take for a woman to be ready to go out, or how much washing of faces, hands and clothes now had to be done. She even made him have a bath even though it wasn't Candlemas or Easter.

She had been quite sweet to him all the time they had been courting but after the honeymoon her character changed. By the Norman law of that time all her wealth became his on the day of the wedding, not that he needed it of course. But she seemed to need so much; not just words of admiration but also dresses, shoes, scarves, combs, brushes and of course cupboards to put them all in. She ordered tables and chairs, curtains and tablecloths, new pots and pans for the kitchen, mirrors for the bedroom and hall, lamps to hang everywhere and thick sumptuous carpets to be laid throughout the house. They soon, he thought, needed a much larger place to live.

One day they were riding back from a shopping trip. They had been at Canterbury market all day and the Arab stallion was weighed down with a carpet, several bolts of cloth, pots and pans and Penny. Even more purchases were packed onto Sam's horse. They were labouring up the long hill of Dover Road towards Bridge when the poor Arab couldn't hold it in any longer.

Now he was a well-bred animal and he was in front. The poor mare was right behind, breathing deeply with the effort of the long climb. The Arab farted causing the mare to snort wildly and say, 'Couldn't you wait?' Sam heard this. He also heard the stallion say, 'You wouldn't wait if you were carrying a great load like this old fat sow and her goods.'

Sam couldn't help himself; he laughed. His wife whipped around in her saddle and demanded to know what he was laughing at. Sam stopped laughing and was about to obediently reply when he realised that if he did reply his head would explode into a thousand pieces. He looked around desperately and pointed to a distant cottage,

'Um, look at that chimney – all bent – have you seen anything so funny in your life?'

Penny scowled. 'Nothing funny about that chimney – nothing funny at all. I think you were laughing at me.'

'Well I – er, I can't tell you. Something terrible would happen if I did tell you. I am sorry.'

'Sorry?! Sorry?? I will make you sorry. You wait 'til I get you home.'

At home they did not speak. He unloaded the shopping, stabled the horses and fed the chickens while she cooked their dinner. She did sound quite cheerful when she called out, 'Food', but he was wary as he sat down at the table. Holding the hot plate with a cloth she served him two succulent pork chops, a few crispy roast potatoes, small heaps of carrots and peas, all with savoury gravy. Sam's mouth watered; this was just the thing, he thought, after a day trailing around the market. He picked up the knife and fork – and his dinner vanished.

In its place there arrived a cracked plate, he recognised it as the one he usually used to feed scraps to the dogs. On it were two dirty bacon rinds, some fluffy burnt fried egg whites and an onion skin.

'And that's all you'll get 'til you tell me why you were laughing,' snapped his wife.

Sam went to bed that night with an empty stomach. He was eventually drifting into dreams of sausages when a voice right in his ear screeched,

'What were you laughing at?'

He shot bolt upright in bed. He was awake enough not to tell her, so she let him settle down under the feather bedspread and she waited. When the church clock struck she did it again. Every hour until dawn she carried on; she could sleep later the next day while he did his shepherding.

Over the next week Sam grew thinner with hollow eyes and a haunted look. Every night's sleep was disturbed; every meal was inedible. He caught sight of himself in one of the new mirrors and thought he had seen a ghost; pale cheeks and thin lips stretched over the bones of his skull. This can't go on, he thought, something must be done. On Friday morning he rode into Woolage and spoke to the builder. Three days later the builder and his man arrived with their cart and put up a pair of trestles outside Sam's house. Then, as instructed, on them they laid a well-made wooden coffin.

Penny burst out of the front door and shouted at the builder. 'What are you doing putting a coffin outside of my house? Who has died?'

'No-one as far as I knows, mam. We was ordered this on Friday by your husband. It's all paid for.'

'I don't care if it is paid for or not – I don't want it. No-one has died around here. Take it away right now.'

'Sorry Mam, we was paid good money to make this and paid good money to deliver it; we was neither ordered nor paid to take it away. So here it stays. Besides which, it were custom made for one particular person, we might have to wait a long time to find another body to fit this.'

'And which particular person was this designed to fit, then? Me?'

'No Mam, it's too narrow for the likes of you. No, it were designed to fit your husband. We measured him up. He told us he was to die today.'

'Sam! Come out here. I know you're in the shed. What's all this about?' Sam walked up to her with the shepherd dogs at his heels.

'It's all about tidiness, that's what it is,' said Sam evenly.

'Tidiness?! What's tidy about a nasty coffin in our front yard?'

Sam took a deep breath. 'Well, you know how you won't let me sleep nor eat properly until I tell you why I laughed on the hill out of Canterbury?'

'Yes? Well?'

'And you remember that I told you something terrible would happen if I told you why I was laughing?'

'Yes, yes, I remember.'

'The terrible thing would be – my head bursting into a thousand pieces so I thought if I was in a coffin when I told you the pieces wouldn't make such a mess all over the yard and you wouldn't have so much to clear up and you could just nail down the coffin lid and forget all about me.' He ran out of breath.

The proud cockerel wandered over to the mother sheepdog. 'I see your old master is going to tell her then. Nice. Fresh meat spread all over the yard when he does; lovely. If she were one of my hens there would be no argument; one good pecking and she would know where she stood.'

The shepherd dog's ears pricked up. 'What was this? The Master dying? But he's the best Master any dog can have. My son and I have had a better life than many a hound in these parts; any problem and the Master knows all about it. He can't just die.' She yelped for her pup to come but couldn't wait for him and met him halfway to the field.

'Now pin back your lugholes and hark. Run fast as you can up to the Great Rock and find the King of the Snakes. Tell him about the Master and the secret and his poor head and ask if the Master's life can be saved. Go now and go quick.'

The dog raced up the hill and disappeared under the hill. Sam had just lain down in the coffin under the scornful eye of his wife and said a few prayers under his breath. He prayed for his soul, he prayed for the health of the dogs, his horse and his sheep and he even added a little one for the soul of his wife.

The King of the Snakes gazed down at the trembling sheepdog.

'Thtate your bithineth, dog,' lisped the King.

'Well, my mum says that our master, Sam the shepherd, came to you some years ago and you allowed him to understand animals.'

'Thith ith true, I did,' admitted the King.

'But now he's going to tell his wife and his head will burst and he's too nice for that to happen and can you do anything to stop it?' said the young dog all in one breath.

'Thtop it?' said the King, 'you want me to thtop it? If he tellth a human there ith'nt much I can do. But wait, there is thomething. Your mathter could be thaved. Leave it to me.'

The King of Snakes closed his eyes and said no more. The dog backed slowly out of the cave and then ran as fast as possible back to Sam's yard. He was shocked to hear Sam saying, 'Wife, would you lift the coffin lid and place it over me? Leave enough space to hear what I'm about to say. Ready? Right. This is why I was laughing that day.' He took a deep breath. 'You see, I can understand what animals are saying.'

He stopped and waited for his head to burst. Nothing happened.

'One day I saved a snakes' life and his father gave me the languages of all the birds and animals. Your fine horse said something so funny on that hill that I had to laugh.' Sam looked at his wife as she leaned over the coffin to listen. 'Your half Arab compared you to a fat old sow.'

'What?! What do you say? What?' Spittle flew out of Penny's mouth and sprayed over Sam's face. 'Whatwhatwhatwhat what? Wirtwirt wirt wirt wirt. But… But… Book book book buk buk buk.'

In front of Sam's surprised face her nose extended into a beak, her hair became a hen's comb, her clothes became feathers and she shrank to the size and shape of one of the cockerel's hen-wives. With a loud clucking she joined the flock of hens. The King of Snakes had devised a just transformation. And Sam still hadn't told another human being; he had told a hen.

So Sam kept his head and his wife became a very lowly hen amongst the dozens that grubbed in the yard. As a newcomer she smelled wrong and was bullied by the other fowl. If she so much as looked at a piece of grain that the cockerel wanted, she got a pecking.

Sam was seen with girl after girl after that but he never remarried. He became a popular and prosperous man of the area. And they changed the name of the village – Sibertswold is now known as Shepherdswell – and now you can guess why.

Twenty-two

THE APPLE-TREE
MAN

Many years ago, near the village of Headcorn, half-way between Maidstone and Tenterden, there was a good farmer who was the eldest of three brothers. When their father died the solicitor read them the will that he had left; a will that was curiously unfair. The farm had been divided unevenly; the youngest boy had been the favourite and had been left nearly everything; the fields, all the barns, the new farmhouse and the cattle. All these he shared out amongst himself and his best friend the middle brother. But the least favoured eldest inherited only an old donkey, a thin ox, a few ancient apple trees and the old tumbledown farm cottage where the family had lived for generations.

Now the older brother didn't grumble about his share, it wasn't his way; he just cut grass from the roadside for the donkey and fattened the ancient animal up. Then he rubbed the old ox with herbs and said 'the words' and the ox grew, month by month, livelier and full of health. He put them both to graze under the old apple trees and what they left behind nourished the roots and made the fruit come again. But he was still using land that belonged to his younger brother who demanded a stiff monthly rent; a rent which often could not be easily found.

One mid-winter's day the youngest brother came into the orchard and jealously admired the animals and the fruit trees. He was a devious and spoilt man and so he said:

Listen. Tomorrow is Christmas Eve; the one day in the year when at midnight the animals can talk. Now, our old Gran used to say that on that holy day at the striking of the midnight hour these animals must speak if asked. I remember our dad once saying there was wonderful treasure buried hereabouts and I believe that the donkey is so old that he may have seen it being hidden. They can't refuse at such a sacred moment. I want to talk with them but you know me; I shall be certain to be in the pub and a little ale is sure to pass my lips. So you be sure to wake me in time to ask them animals about the treasure tomorrow night, say about quarter to twelve. You do that and I'll knock sixpence off your rent. Right? Will you do that?

The older brother said he would.

The next day the donkey and the ox were given a little extra to eat and a bough of holly was fixed up over their shed. The older brother took the last of his cider and put it in a tin to mull in the

ashes of the fire before taking it out to give it to the apple trees. As the animals silently watched he poured the steaming alcohol over the roots and wished the spirits of the trees to be generous with their fruit in the next year. As the pungent brew sunk into the soil a strong deep voice was heard calling from all around: 'I am the Apple-Tree Man, the spirit of the trees. I thank you for the libation. Look under my great diddicky root and you will find a chest of much gold. 'Tis yours and belongs to no one else. Put it away safe and keep quiet about it.'

The farmer was frightened at first and then curious. He searched warily behind the trees but there was no one playing tricks on him. So he went back to his old cottage and found a mattock and he had soon unearthed an old chest, which he took and hid carefully where none would find it. When he returned to the trees to collect the animals the Apple-Tree Man spoke again.

'Now 'tis nearly midnight and time to waken your brother. Farewell until the seasons do turn again.'

The animals were led into their shed and settled down for the rest of the night. The older brother took himself off to the new farmhouse to set about rousing his brother. Now it was nearly midnight. When the younger brother was awakened he rushed down the path and into the shed to hear what the animals might say. The church clock in the distance chimed the midnight hour. He heard the donkey talking to the ox:

'Hee-haw, you know that greedy brother who is listening so rudely to us now? He wants us to tell him where his great-grandfather's gold is buried.'

'Is that so?' said the ox, 'well, he'll never get it. 'Cos someone has taken it already.'

The elder brother used the fortune wisely and had a happy life, but the younger brother cursed and dug the land for the rest of his days.

Twenty-three

BRAVE MARY
OF MILL HILL

There was a time when every town and village had a mill for grinding flour from seed. Sometimes there were two mills; a windmill on the hill to catch the wind in the sails and a watermill beside the river or stream with its wheel in the flowing water. Every hill with a mill was called 'Mill Hill', whilst 'Mill Stream's or 'Mill Ponds' are still to be found everywhere long after the machinery has disappeared.

Mill Hill in Deal had a mill at the top and living in it was a miller and his feisty daughter. The miller was a lazy man who used the mill sail cogs to pull up the heavy bags of grain to the top of the mill and there he tipped the seeds into a hopper where a bell would ping when the hopper was empty. A deeper bell would sound when the grain had been through the mill wheels, been ground to flour and the sack below was full. He would then stroll down and change the full sack for an empty one.

All week long he would mill flour but on Sunday nights, after church, he would sit in his mill with the carpenter and play cards. The miller always won most of the money but the carpenter never complained. He was always too addled. One gulp of beer, a single sip of wine or just the smell of brandy would send his head spinning.

'Deuce of Hearts beats Knave of Spades,' he would cry – but it never did. Until one fateful week when the miller forgot to buy any booze. This was a disaster. The coins went steadily across the table to the carpenter's side until they formed a pretty large heap. The miller needed to find some alcohol for the carpenter soon before he was driven into poverty.

Now, the alehouse was at the bottom of Mill Hill. In those days to get there you had to walk down the 'Witches Path' through an ancient orchard that was very overgrown and dark. Everyone knew that it was haunted, as was the graveyard further down. The bodies were in the clay above the chalk; when the rain was heavy the clay would slip and roll skeleton arms and heads up through the ground. Then there was the ghastly crypt beneath the church. Even the Vicar didn't like to go down there amongst the skulls and bones of the priests from years before. It, too, was known to be haunted.

Now neither man liked to go down the hill even in broad daylight. But the miller knew that all would be lost unless he could find some alcohol to stem his friend's good fortune.

'Mary,' the miller shouted, 'bring yourself up here.'

'Coming, Father,' sounded a chirpy reply. Her nimble shoes clattered up the wooden stairs and there she was, bright-faced and sixteen years old. The miller looked at her gravely.

'Mary my dear, would you take a few coins down to the alehouse and fetch us some beer? You're not afraid of the Witches Path, are you?'

Mary looked at him with a steady eye. ''Course not. Give me the coins, then.'

The carpenter said, 'But then there is the graveyard, my dear. And after that you must pass close by the crypt of the church. Don't ghosties scare you at all?'

She laughed. 'Why should they scare me? They're only spirits. I just remember what my great-grandma once said, "They are dead and you're alive and that's an end to it, so thppppptht."

She put her tongue between her lips and blew a wet raspberry to show her distain. 'I'll take these pennies, shall I?'

The carpenter wiped his face. Mary picked up the money and ran down the stairs. She sang 'la la la' as she skipped down the dark

Witches Path ignoring the bats and the branches snagging at her clothes. The graveyard got some cheerful 'de de des' as well, as did the creepy crypt full of bones. When she reached the alehouse she bought the beer and then went 'tra la la' all the way back up the hill to the mill.

'Well, you are the fearless one, aren't you? Does nothing make you afraid?' asked the carpenter.

'I told you before. They are dead and I'm alive and that's an end to it, so thppppptht.'

'You are very rude,' spluttered the carpenter, wiping his face, 'I bet you, I bet you're not brave enough to go into that crypt next Sunday night and bring me back – um – a skull. I bet you two whole pounds you can't do that.' He was rudely jabbing at her with his finger while he said this but she reached out and grabbed it, shook it and said, 'The bet is on!'

All the way home that night the carpenter worried about what he had done. She was too brave; he would lose two whole pounds. That was more than he could sometimes earn in a week. The next morning he had an idea and he called in at the Parsonage to see the Vicar. The holy man owed him money and when he answered the door he was in rather a fluster.

'I am s..s..so sorry, my good c..c..carpenter, but I cannot p..p.. pay you this month. There has been nothing in the c..c..collecting plate but b..b..buttons and s..s..stones for weeks.'

The carpenter smiled at him. 'Your worries on that score are over, if you will do a little favour for me.'

'W..w..what favour do you m mean, my good man?'

'Well, next Sunday night young Mary, the miller's daughter, will creep into your crypt and try to steal a skull.'

'W..w..why would she do that?' spluttered the Vicar.

'It's just a silly bet, don't worry about it. All you have to do is find yourself an old bed sheet, cut a couple of eye holes in it, go down to the crypt just before midnight, and wait. When Mary comes in you waft the sheet about and make some ghostly noises. Mary will run away with no skull and I'll let you off all the money you owe me. Is that a deal?'

The Vicar turned a little paler. 'I..I am not sure. It's very c..c.. creepy down there. All those b..b..bones.'

'Five minutes, that's all it will be, Vicar.' The carpenter smiled again encouragingly.

So it was that just before midnight the next Sunday night the Vicar, under his sheet, hid down in the crypt. He was sweaty and scared as he heard 'la la la' coming closer and closer. The crypt door creaked on rusty hinges and Mary felt her way down the stone steps, not worrying about the cobwebs and slugs that her fingers met on the way. She groped about until she touched a skull and she picked it up.

Up came the Vicar with the sheet over his head. 'Whooo-ooh-woooogh! Leave it alone. That is the skull of my Grandfather. Woooogh!'

'Oh, I'm so sorry,' said Mary and she put the skull down with a plonk. Her fingers found another skull and she picked it up.

Up came the Vicar again. 'Whoo-woooogh! Leave it alone. That is the skull of my great-grandfather. Woooogh!'

'So very sorry, I'm sure,' said Mary, 'I'll try another.' She lifted another skull and up came the Vicar again.

The Vicar said, 'Wooooogh! Leave it…'

'Shut up with your "wooos", you silly spirit,' interrupted Mary, 'For I must have a skull for it is a bet, you see?' Without another word she turned and took the skull up the steps and out of the crypt, locking the door behind her like any good girl should. With a careless trill of 'la la la's she took the skull up the Mill Hill.

When she arrived at the windmill the carpenter was upset to see that his plan had failed. He begrudgingly took the skull and paid Mary the two gold coins and said, 'You did get this from the crypt, didn't you? You didn't dig in the graveyard, did you?'

'Oh no, I went into the smelly old crypt all right,' said Mary.

'And wasn't there a fearsome ghost in that Crypt?'

'Yes there was – but there is nothing to fear. It moaned about its grandfather and its great-grandfather but I locked the door on the way out so it couldn't follow.'

'You locked the door? Oh no. Come with me, miller, and quick as you can. We may be too late.'

They ran down that Witches Path, flew past the graveyard and unlocked the crypt door. They were too late; the Vicar lay on his back with his eyes staring up at the crypt ceiling, his hair snowy white and standing on end. He had scared himself to death.

The story of the Vicar's death and Mary's bravery spread through Deal and Walmer, Kingsdown and Guston. It soon came to the ears of the Squire of Dover, who was very interested. Not in the dead Vicar, nothing unusual there. No, the squire had a problem with a ghost in his fine mansion; a ghost that had scared away all the servants.

You see, his mother had recently died but that wasn't the worst of it. She hadn't told him where she had hidden all the money. Worse than that, she hadn't left the mansion. Her ghostly wraith would float through the walls, scaring away all the servants. For instance, the cook was stirring the porridge one morning when a spirit head loomed up out of the pot. Cook flew out of the door in a cloud of flour, ran off the Dover cliffs and made her way to Portugal. The groom was rubbing down the stallion's flank one day when he felt a mouth in the horsehair, then an eye and a nose. He let out a piercing scream and ran all the way to Ramsgate where he leapt off the cliffs and swam all the way to Belgium.

Soon the squire was all alone in the house with no one to either cook or clean. He had never before in his life been without servants. He didn't know how to cook, get dressed, clean his own teeth (the servants used to hold the toothbrush against his teeth while another would grab his ears and swivel his head back and forth) or even wipe his own bottom. Getting dressed took him a long while every morning; buttons were fiddly and trousers were complicated. He tried hanging his trousers on the drawer knobs and jumping into them with bruising results; sometimes both his legs would jam into one trouser leg and sometimes he missed altogether. He desperately needed help and now there was news of a brave young girl who may fit the bill. He made his way to Mill Hill, Deal. He found the miller and put a proposal to him.

'I understand, miller, that your daughter is afraid of nothing. I have a position waiting for her in my haunted Dover mansion, a position worth ten gold guineas a year. Send her to my house immediately.'

'I'm so sorry, sir, I beg your pardon but you will have to ask her yourself. She's a wilful young thing with a mind of her own.' He called down the stairs. 'Mary, come here.'

Mary skipped in to the room and looked the squire in the eye. The squire repeated the offer to her, 'Will you come to my haunted mansion for ten whole gold guineas a year, m'dear?'

'No, I won't,' said bold Mary.

'So, the ghost would keep even Brave Mary of Mill Hill away. Not so brave now, are you?'

'Oh no, it's not the ghost that will keep me away, for they are dead and I'm alive and that's an end to it, so thppppptht.'

The squire wiped his face.

Mary looked knowingly at the Squire. 'No, you shall have to pay me twenty whole gold guineas a year for I have heard that no one else will work for you.'

She was right; he couldn't find anyone else. He reluctantly agreed to the twenty guineas, put her on his horse and took her home.

So it was that Mary moved into the mansion and all went very well. She curtsied to the spirit each morning when it arrived, she laid a place for it at the table, making sure she never crossed the silver cutlery (for crossed silver will keep the undead away) and made up a bed for it each night complete with wash jug and bowl. She cooked and cleaned and taught the squire to do a few personal things for himself. The squire grew to admire and like her, although she was only a peasant girl.

One morning the squire said, 'Mary my dear, I must go away to Maidstone on business. I will be gone for two days; but the spirit is still about. Will you be alright here on our own?'

'Of course I will,' she said, 'I've told you before, they are dead and I'm alive and that's an end to it, so thpppptht."

'So you did, so you did. Well, I must be off. Farewell, my dear. I will be back on Thursday. Bye bye.' He wiped his face, mounted his horse and off he rode.

The next morning Mary had her back to the door as she swept the ashes from the fireplace, so she did not notice the green-grey mist that flowed under the door and across the floor. It mounded itself up until there was the vague form of the squire's mother. An eerie wailing voice filled the room.

'Maree, Maree, are you afraid of meeeee?'

Mary turned round and faced the wraith, 'No I'm not,' she said firmly.

'Why are you not afraid of meeeee?' asked the spirit.

'Well it's like this. You are dead and I'm alive and that's an end to it, so thpppptht.'

The ghost wiped her eyes. 'Mary, I have a task for you to do in the cellar. Follow meeeee.'

'Shall I bring a candle? It's very dark down there.'

'Noooo,' moaned the ghost, 'I shall light the way myself.'

The wraith of the squire's mother lit up from inside like a lantern, so that you could see her ribs, her heart and even what she had eaten for dinner the day she died. Mary followed her glowing form down the cellar steps, first to the right and then to the left and looked at where the spirit finger was pointing. There was a stone slab in the floor with an iron ring set in it.

'Maree, lift the ring.'

Mary pulled on the ring and the heavy stone slab lifted to reveal a hollow space beneath. In the space were two hessian sacks, a little one and a big one.

'Maree, will you remember a message to my son?'

'I'm a clever girl with a good mind. I will remember your message. What is it?'

'Woooooh,' wailed the ghost, 'here is the message from beyond the grave: "My dearest child. The large sack contains much gold. With Mary's help you will spend it wisely, my son. The little sack of gold is for Mary, for being so brave." Woooooh. I must now go to the world beyond. Tell my son the message, my dear.'

'I will, of course,' stated Mary.

'Then my work on Earth is done,' screeched the squire's mother's wraith, and in a swirl of vapour she disappeared.

When the squire returned Mary told him of the unearthly visit and that it had brought good news of the missing money. 'I will show you, down in the cellar. Bring a candle,' she asked, 'for it is mighty dark down there.'

Mary lead the way down the steps and the squire admired her long, dark hair in the candlelight. Her shapely bottom impressed him when she bent over to pull on the iron ring in the stone slab. Her voice was sweet to his ears when she said,

'Here is a message from your dear, dead mother from beyond the grave. It goes like this: "Woooooh. The small sack contains gold that with Marys help you will spend wisely. The large sack is for Mary for being so brave, Woooooh." That's all she said before she vanished for ever to be with Jesus.'

So that the ghost could never return Mary always made sure that she crossed the cutlery at every meal and she put ivy around the doors to bar ethereal beings from entry. Mary was a servant yet also a very rich girl.

But the squire was sweet on Mary and after a year they were married. The law in those days was that any property owned by the wife became the husband's property on the day of the wedding. So he had his money back in the end. And he had a clever, beautiful wife – which is probably as close to a happy ending as we can get.

Twenty-four

GREY LADY WOODS

If you were travelling from Deal to Dover along the A258 you would leave Walmer and travel south-west through Ringwould, then descend through a snaking, wooded bend at the bottom of the hill before climbing the curving hill to pass the turnings left to St Margarets at Cliffe and right to Martin Mill. You would have just passed through Grey Lady Woods in Oxney Bottom. Why 'Grey Lady' you may ask?

There have been several accounts of apparitions, appearances and disappearances over the years: There was the ghost of an honourable highwayman who never robbed from women but was nevertheless hanged nearby; a lady in grey standing at the crossroads who vanished when approached; an ancient coach and horses that burst from the woods on one side of the road and crossed to enter the trees opposite. A boy, who fell down a well, could not be rescued and his body was left there when the well was filled in; his spirit still apparently haunts the area. In the 1950s a double-decker bus picked up an old lady who could be heard climbing the stairs to the top deck yet could not be found by the conductor, a Mr Tom Relf, a minute later despite the bus not having stopped.

Yet the strangest tale concerns a caring driver and an unusual hitch-hiker. The driver, a lecturer at a local college, was heading from Dover towards Deal late one dim winter's afternoon through driving rain and feeling thankful that he would soon be at home by a crackling log fire. As he reached the Grey Lady Woods he saw a bare arm gesturing from the side of the road; not thumbing but waiving. His headlights were spattered with mud but he could see a slight figure with long dark hair cowering from the rain.

He picked up hitch-hikers when he could. Many years ago as a student he had hitch-hiked around most of Britain and some of Europe with fair success, yet he still remembered some cold lonely spots where the few drivers who passed had either stared fixedly ahead or indicated with a pointing finger that they would soon be turning off. So since he had owned a car he had picked up hitch-hikers whenever he saw them with the thought, 'What goes around comes around.' He braked and stopped a few yards beyond the figure, leaned across the passenger seat and opened the door.

The rear passenger door was opened and a wet, cold girl got in. Her voice was light and faint as she said, 'Me Mum says I should always sit in the back for safety. Sorry. I don't mean to seem unfriendly.' The car filled with the scent of patchouli oil.

'That's quite all right, you sit where you like,' said the driver as he closed the passenger door, 'how far are you going? You look chilled to the bone.'

The girl sniffed. 'Me Mum lives in Mongeham, Oakenfield, big house at the bottom of the hill on the right just before the playing field. Hope it's not too far out of your way.' Her teeth chattered as she spoke and the driver realised how lightly dressed she was for the weather.

'I can go straight past it on my way to Northbourne,' said the driver, 'why don't you put my jacket on, keep yourself warm.' He picked up his tweed jacket and passed it back over the seats. He pulled away and watched her in the rear-view mirror as she draped the jacket round her shoulders.

'You should really dress a bit warmer for this weather. But I know it's no good telling you young people – It's all fashion and "street cred" these days.'

There was no reply from the back seat. He glanced in the rear-view mirror. Her head was bowed and her hair hung in front of her face – perhaps she is sleepy, he thought.

'Student, are you? At the college in Dover?'

There was still no reply. He drove on through Upper Walmer, swung left into Station Road and under the railway bridge along the narrow Ellens Road. He passed the dog kennels and the cattery before turning right into village. He drove past the playing field in Mongham and parked just beyond the village hall outside a double fronted house. He couldn't see a name plaque. He glanced into the mirror, 'Is this your Mum's house, then?'

He couldn't see her so he swung round and looked into the back of the car. The car was empty, the plastic seat cover showing a damp patch where the girl had sat. He hadn't stopped since picking her up; there was no way that she could have left the car without him noticing, for the rusty doors of his creaky old Peugeot were never silent to open nor to close.

He got out of the car and walked round it, staring down the rain swept road he had just travelled along. He shook his head to clear it. Where had she gone? Now he could see that behind a yew hedge was the house name in faded paint; 'Oakenfield'. He had better tell the mother that he had given her daughter a lift, even if she had disappeared.

The gravel crunched under his feet as he approached the porch. The heavy door sported both an electric bell and a tarnished brass knocker in the shape of Minerva. As it was now very dark it may seem threatening to knock, he felt. He pressed the button of the bell. He could hear a faint buzz from deep in the house. He waited.

The woman who opened the door was probably in her fifties, narrow faced and not particularly friendly. 'We don't buy anything at the door,' she snapped and started to close it. The driver managed to say, 'It's about your daughter, I've just given her a lift,' before the door closed. The door swung open again. The woman's face was now unreadable; a mixture of despair and grief overlaid with resignation.

'If that's the case you had better give me a lift up the hill. You did lend her your coat or something, didn't you?'

'Well, yes, I did. She wasn't dressed for this weather, you know.'

'She never is,' the woman said, shrugging on a raincoat and heading for the car.

'So where are we going?'

'St Martin's Church, off the Northbourne road. I'll explain on the way.' The woman installed herself in the passenger seat and fastened the seatbelt.

The driver got in, turned the car round and headed up the hill towards Northbourne. He tried a little light conversation. 'She is very careful, your daughter. She said you told her to get in the back of a car as it was safer, and she did.'

'Hmm.'

'I come past here most days but I'm not sure I know where the church is. Sorry.'

'Next on the right.'

He turned the car into a narrow lane and up to a stone church set at an angle to the road.

'Come on,' said the woman getting out, 'I expect you have been wondering where she got to. She's just through here.'

He followed her to the right of the church then off the church path to walk amongst a scattering of gravestones and monuments; some old and worn but others crisply carved and recent. Some sported bunches of flowers while others seemed grown over and neglected. The woman stopped in front of a fairly new stone cross. 'Here we are.'

The driver could see something round the cross. The woman was hunched forward, her shoulders heaving as sobs burst from her. 'This is where my daughter lives now. If only she would stay here but time and again she gets a lift, trying to come home, I suppose. There's her name there.'

She pointed to the engraved words on the cross:

In Loving Memory
of
EMILY SANDERS
Taken from us 12th November 1987 aged twenty-two.

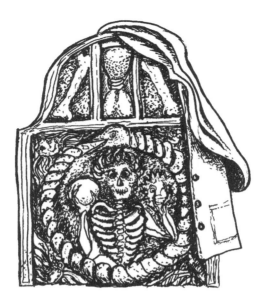

'And I expect that's your jacket, is it?'

It was his jacket draped round the cross, soaking wet but with nothing missing from the pockets. It smelled quite strongly of patchouli oil.

Twenty-five

A KINGSDOWN ROMANCE

The white cliffs of Dover stretch north-northwest from Capel-le-Ferne past Abbots Cliff and Shakespeare's Cliff (where King Lear raved) to Dover; past Langton, Fan and Crab Bays to St Margaret's Bay. On they tower to Hope Point and then they bow down at Kingsdown to touch the stony beach at Oldstairs Bay. They are much as they have always been; some chalk has fallen and a few more tunnels have been dug through them but they stand defiantly facing France as they have done since the great sea-quake washed away the land bridge to Cap Gris-Nez.

It was around 200 years ago that a wrecked boat rested on the shingle beach below the cliffs at Old Parkers Cap, Oldstairs Bay, Kingsdown. It had been made into a small home with two narrow windows, a curved door and a thatched roof of reeds that sported a small chimney. In it, alone, lived Tom the fisherman. He would go out in his fishing boat on the high tide just like the other fishermen of Walmer and Deal and return just as they did on the next high tide. They would all catch cod, sole and plaice off the Goodwin Sands and sell them on trestle tables set out on Walmer Strand near the beach. The rest of the fishermen would carry their takings to a pub and spend the money on beer, tobacco, gambling and food;

they would tell tales and sing songs and if any money was left it would go home to their wives.

But Tom lived alone. What made him want to be such a solitary creature no one knew, but he seldom spoke to anyone and never visited the pub. Yet still he sang. When the tide had taken the breaking waves far from the cliffs he would walk to the water's edge and sing to the great wall of chalk. He had a strong rich baritone voice and his notes and words would echo back to harmonise with him:

'Oh, mee name is Tommmm'

Back would come the echo, just as he sang the second line.

'Oh, mee name is Tommmm'
'I am a fishermannnnn'

His voice and his echo would blend together, for his harmonic melody would take any of the five notes and combine them naturally with each other. One spring night the moon was high and fat making the chalk faces glow. The waves were breaking far from the cliffs and Tom had to wait longer than usual for his echo to return. When it did there was something strange about it; another voice had joined his and its echo. The notes were sweet and true, a low sweet female sound enhancing his harmonies, dancing between them:

'Oh, his name is Tommmm'

Tom paused a moment, took a deep breath and sang the second line.

'I am a fishermannnnn'

The delicate voice sang out in accord back from the cliff

'He is such a fishermannnnn'

Tom sang on, walking towards the chalk, revelling in the sensation of the harmonies. Each time the notes would return sooner and louder. His heart would beat stronger and he felt his face warming. Were these, he thought, the sensations of being in love? No one falls in love with just a voice, do they? But he was drawn closer and closer to the sound as if by invisible threads wrapped around his soul. The sweet voice was closer, louder. The words were new:

⸱His song is the song of my own tender heart⸲

As Tom rounded a shoulder of chalk he saw a young woman sitting on a rock. He froze, keeping utterly still and silent. It was not a figure that he recognised. Her back was to him but he could see in the bright moonlight that she wore no clothes over her pale skin. Her only garment lay in a crumpled heap beside the rock; it was composed of tiny scales of grey, blue, silver and green and was in the form of a long fish tail. Down her back flowed cascades of silvery-green hair. He could see her eyelashes beyond her high cheekbones and the way her neck flowed into her back like some finely carved figurehead. Tom felt dizzy; it seemed to him that his heart would burst. She was a mermaid. They were shy creatures by all accounts; if he startled her she would slip away back through the pools and into the salt waves in a flash. He could not let that happen. He may never see her again. And he – yes he loved her.

Now Tom was neither a young man nor the most graceful of fishermen. Yet he moved across the loose shingle towards that mermaid without making a single sound. Not a pebble rattled, not a shell scraped. When he could reach the mermaids tail he snatched it up and thrust it inside his jacket. A few small stones clicked together, a tiny shell rattled and the mermaid spun around and faced him with her arms across her chest. Her voice was low, sweet and liquid.

'Please give me my garment, for without it I cannot swim in the sea with my friends and family.'

She pleaded with arms spread. Now that he could see her deep blue eyes his heart lurched against his ribs. He took a deep breath and he spoke: 'My darling, I believe that I have fallen in love with you. Forgive me, but I would like to make you a cup of tea in my home back there.' His thumb jerked over his shoulder towards the upturned boat. 'I promise you that once you have shared my tea you shall have your garment back. You have only to ask for it. I cross my heart that you shall have it if it is asked for.'

Without waiting for a reply he turned his back on her and crunched across the shingle towards his thatched boat. He knew that he must follow him, without her garment what else could she do? He heard her little cries behind him as the sharp stones and shells dug into her tender new feet. He reached the door and stood outside holding it open for her to enter.

'After you, my lady,' he invited.

As she stepped in he thrust her garment deep into the reed thatch above where she would never find it.

The mermaid sat at the table and her eyes widened as she watched Tom fill the kettle from the jug and put it on the pot-bellied stove.

'What are you doing?' she asked.

'Why, simply heating the water for the tea, my dear.'

'And what is that glowing like a setting sun from beneath?'

'That is a fire to heat the water, my precious.'

'What is fire? We have nothing so lovely under the sea.'

Tom explained that trees give wood, which is allowed to dry, and that a flame will set it ablaze to give heat. The mermaid smiled. It was a smile that could stop a heart. Tom smiled too.

'And what is this "tea" that you are making?'

As Tom described the distant lands of India and China where tea grew and the tea bushes whose leaf tips were taken, her smile grew wider. She giggled when Tom told her of the ships that brought it thousands of miles to England and of the rich merchants who bought it, graded it, packaged it and sold it at high prices. When he said that it was put into hot water for a minute or two then thrown away she laughed helplessly for a long while. Tom had to laugh with her although he didn't know what she was laughing at.

'That is the silliest thing I have ever heard,' she spluttered, 'all that work and you throw it away.'

'Well then, what is it that mermaids drink at the bottom of the sea?' asked Tom.

The mermaid laughed again showing even white teeth.

'We are immersed in water; we have no need of drink.'

They conversed for hours about life below and above the waves. He made her fish supper and still she did not ask for her garment. She shared his bed. He found her some clothes and shoes and the next morning he walked with her on the beach. He showed her his fishing boat and when she saw his nets she shuddered. He held her close as she explained that many a mermaid, merman or merchild had been caught in such nets and had died of their struggles. He took care not to show her the lines with the barbed hooks.

Days passed and turned into weeks that became months. She never asked for the garment and her belly grew with a baby. When he was born, Little Tom had tiny webs between his fingers and toes and a pulse behind each ear where gills might have been. A year later a baby sister joined them. They called her Perri. She, too, had the webs and the pulses but like Little Tom the pulses faded and the webs did not grow with the fingers or toes. They played with other Kingsdown children; running, catching, dancing and singing. At swimming no other child could compete with either of them.

Their mermaid mother showed them the secrets of the sea and shore; how to find flints that rang like a xylophone, how to read the tides and currents, how to make a paper kite that floated in the air like a bird of prey and teased the grey seals into thinking there was a shoal of fish below.

The mermaid seemed content, although one bright afternoon Little Tom saw her at the sink before the window with tears shining in her eyes. The wind was skimming the tops of the waves and the spray was making rainbows above each one. He grasped her legs and asked her what was wrong and if he could help. Her sapphire eyes regarded him and she softly said:

Little one, there are times when something must be lost when something is gained. When I came to love your father I gained much, a kind man and two sweet children, but I lost more than I ever knew I had. These tears are for both having and for not having.

Little Tom did not understand this but he held her tighter and it seemed to help. Years went by, the children grew and Tom fished the Channel in his boat.

One autumn night in the sea off the coast of Spain, at a place once called Finisterre, which means 'End of the World', cold air met warm air and wet air met dry and it all boiled up into a howling storm. It blasted up the English Channel blowing Tom and the other fishermen past the Low Countries along the Danish coast to the Skagerrak straits south of Norway. The winds at last dropped and the fishermen were left with torn sails, broken masts, smashed rudders and missing friends.

They took three days and nights to limp back to the Kent coast. They arrived on a bright sunny morning; the low eastern sun blazing through the air, freshened by the storm, bleaching the cliffs. As Tom beached, his eye caught sight of something shiny on the roof of his hut. Walking closer he could see that the reeds had been blown off by the storm had exposed his wife's garment. It glistened like a bed of jewels; blue, silver and green. So many years ago he had hidden it; he had almost forgotten that it was there. It must be hidden again, Tom thought, for if she finds it she may be gone.

But other eyes had seen the wonderful tail. Halfway up the Oldstairs Steps that climbed the cliff was Little Tom with a large green cricket on his finger. He watched his father take the bejewelled garment down from the thatch and hide it behind the thatched boat under some old nets. He saw his father collect his tools and return to the fishing boat to do some repairs. He put the cricket back into the grass. He ran down the steps to greet his mother when she returned from market along the lower cliff path and he could not contain his excitement. His words tumbled like splashing water.

'Mother, I have seen something wonderful. It's glistening and sparkly and made of lots of little bits of blue and green and silver like a princess's gown in the stories. Let me show you.'

She smiled but did not say a word. He took her hand and led her behind their home.

No one ever saw that mermaid again. Tom and the young ones missed her terribly. But if one of the children had a birthday, on that night there would be a line of wet footprints stretching from the breaking waves to the child's bed. On the floor by the bed would be a pool of water. It could have been seawater dripped from a mermaid's body; it could have been tears. It could have been either, for both are salty.

Twenty-six

THE SEASIDE AND THE LONDONERS: LIL

The East Kent coast; Ramsgate, Margate, Broadstairs, Walmer and Deal became popular leisure destinations when the railway lines arrived around the mid-nineteenth century. For most Londoners the sea was a complete novelty; a wonder to behold. For the wealthy, the salty waters promised health; for the poor, there was amusement.

There was a London housewife, Lil, who made up her mind to see the sea. Her neighbour saw her early one summer morning outside her front door. She was wearing her best frock and hat and was carrying a large bag and an umbrella. The neighbour couldn't help asking where she was going.

'I'm off for a day out,' came the reply. 'It's me first since me hubby died and I need to cheer meself up. I'm going on the railway train down to Margate in Kent. Have you ever been there? There'll be the sea and beaches and everything. There's even a shell grotto.'

'Crikey, Lil, that's a long way isn't it? How much will it cost you? Have you got your lunch? I've never seen the sea, have you?'

'No, I haven't, so it will be a real experience wont it? The fare is four pence, a ha-penny more than the boat trip but much quicker and not so choppy. I tell you what, find me a little bottle or something and I'll put some seawater in it and bring it back, so you can see what it's like. But hurry up, I've got to get to St Paul's Station yet and the train leaves in an hour.'

Lil caught the train in good time with her lunch and an empty medicine bottle in her huge bag. Soon the locomotive had crossed the Thames and as the train trundled through the city outskirts she was amazed to see into the backs of people's houses; there was washing hanging rudely on lines, pigeon lofts with wheeling flocks, vegetables growing and housework being vigorously done. After the stops at Dartford and Gravesend the train speeded up past fields of cows and sheep, crops growing, past green woods and hedges before it stopped at Chatham then Sittingbourne and Gillingham.

The sea became visible near Whitstable and Lil started to feel excited. With a noisy cloud of steam it came to rest in Margate Station near the beach and Lil stepped down ready for a wonderful day. The air was sparkling fresh and the Margate Sands stretched out with salt waves crashing onto the shore; there were bathing machines, Punch and Judy shows to entertain people and donkeys crowding the beach. She made her way to the Stone Pier and there was a fisherman stacking some fish baskets on his boat. He was on just the same level as her so she decided to speak.

'Good morning,' she said boldly. 'I wonder if you could help me? I am from London, don't you know, and my dear neighbour

is not so well travelled as what I am and she has never seen the sea in her life. She gave me this little bottle and asked me to put some sea-water in it for her to keep, but I am afraid to step into the waves to get it, what with my fine dress and shoes and all. Would you fetch me some? Would it be expensive?'

'Hallo,' thought the fisherman, 'we've got a right one here.'

'No, me dear.' he said, 'sea water ain't costly. A little bottle like that I can fill right up for three farthings. Give it here.'

Lil handed him the bottle and a halfpenny and a farthing so he leaned down over the side of his boat and filled up the bottle, re-corked it and gave it back. She thanked him and carefully placed it into her bag.

Off she went into Margate town proper and had herself a wonderful time. She went to a 'Hall of Mirrors' where she was turned both very fat and painfully thin; she had her photograph taken with her head sticking through a clown cut-out, watched a magician produce a bunch of flowers from nowhere, ate some cockles and mussels with two slices of bread washed down with a cup of tea for lunch and had a dance with a cheeky old sailor who pinched her bum at the Tivoli Dance Hall. She recovered from all this with a gentle stroll around the Ranalagh Pleasure Gardens looking at the flowers and trees before some more tea. Then it was time to catch the train back to London.

On her way to the station she was amazed to see that the sea water had gone from the beach and was now only just visible, the waves breaking far away. She passed the fisherman and his boat again, now low down against the Stone Pier. She leaned over and gave him a piece of her mind.

'You should be ashamed of yourself charging so much for that sea-water. You must have made a king's ransom today. Look at how much you have sold. It must be gallons and gallons you've bottled. I shall write to the Mayor of Margate to complain. You see if I don't.'

With that she flounced off to the station and returned to London.

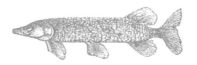

Twenty-seven

THE SEASIDE AND THE LONDONERS: PROPER FISHING

Albert and Cuthbert had been neighbours in London for most of their lives. They had been at Sunday school together, grown up together and took a job together as clerks in the same office. Their wives chatted over the garden fence and their children played together in the adjoining gardens or on the nearby Clapham Common while their fathers went fishing in the Common ponds.

But both men felt that they wanted, for once in their lives, to go what they called 'proper fishing'. They had seen pictures of it in the papers and met people who had done it and they both dreamed of fishing in the salty sea and catching cod, Dover sole, bass, mackerel, or plaice. So their wives were not surprised when their husbands announced that they were going down to Deal in Kent next Saturday to hire a little boat and do 'a bit of proper fishing', as they put it.

For such a special occasion they bought First Class tickets for the train. After all, they wouldn't be doing this very often; they may as well make a good day out of it. At seven in the morning they boarded the train carriage, admired the luxury seating and lit their pipes. Along came the conductor who clipped their tickets, wished them a very pleasant journey and announced that breakfast would be served in the dining car from eight o'clock onwards. Cuthbert asked if the breakfast was included in the First Class tickets and was told that it was. The men smiled, anticipating the beginnings of a fine day.

The dining car smelled and looked wonderful. Spread out and piled up were scrambled eggs, toast, kedgeree, sausages, fried eggs, bacon, pork chops, devilled kidneys, fried bread, porridge, black pudding, fried mushrooms, half-grapefruits, grilled kippers, fried tomatoes, muffins, bubble and squeak and coffee, orange juice and tea. Albert and Cuthbert set to, having their plates filled several times over.

After all, this was their day out. Besides which they had paid for it, hadn't they? Best to make the most of it, eh? They were still eating as the train chuffed down to Dover then along below the White Cliffs towards Martin Mill and Walmer. When they reached Deal Station the two clerks were feeling very full.

Carrying their fishing gear they staggered down Queen Street to the seafront. They soon met a whiskery old fisherman who dubiously agreed to hire them a rowboat for the day. The tide was high and the fisherman helped them launch the boat down the shingle beach into the choppy water, advising that they need not go far from shore as the fish were plentiful everywhere. Cuthbert took the oars, fitted them into the rowlocks and off they went, 'proper fishing' at last.

Albert sat in the back of the craft and watched for France approaching but of course they were too far away and low in the water to see the opposite coast. Besides which this was very different from the ponds and streams in London parks. The water was lumpy. The boat went up and down with the waves and rocked from side to side at the same time. Albert shook his head but the sensations just became worse. He could feel his breakfast slopping about in his stomach and when he remembered the greasy bacon and the runny fried eggs he felt even sicker.

'Can we stop for a minute, Bert, I feel a bit dicky,' asked Albert.

'No stopping now, my friend, it's time to cast your line and see what we can catch. The bait is in that tin between my feet.'

Albert found the tin and prised it open. The live maggots writhed, not something that usually bothered Albert but what with the boat going up and down and rocking from side to side and being so full in the stomach he had no self control left. He leaned over the side of the boat and with a horrible roar all his breakfast spewed into the sea.

'Whoops-a-daisy,' said Cuthbert, 'you'll feel better now.'

'Yesh,' said Albert, 'I do feel better in the shtomach but me teef are in the drink with me breakfasht.'

'What both sets? Upper and lower? That's a bit of a shame. Still, you weren't going to be biting the fish were you? Bait up and cast your line, my friend, there is still fishing to be done,' Cuthbert said encouragingly.

'Don't want to now. The day ish shpoiled for me. How could I eat any fish we catch wiff no teef?' Albert moaned.

'Well, come and take the oars while I cast out, would you?'

They clumsily swapped places and Cuthbert fished while Albert studiously ignored him and all his doings. As they drifted south of the Goodwin Sands Cuthbert felt his line tighten. A big fish by the feel of it. He reeled it in; it was a huge ten pound cod. Partly he felt glad but also he felt sorry for poor old Albert. Then he had an idea. 'I can cheer him up,' he thought, 'maybe the day won't be a complete loss if I could get Albert to smile just once.'

While Albert stared into the distance Cuthbert took his own false teeth out of his mouth, prized open the cod's mouth and fitted them in. They gave the cod a lunatic grin, bound to make Albert laugh. He gave him a nudge.

'Here, cheer up mate, look; this here cod has got your teeth.'

Albert turned to look. No smile crossed his face. He reached out and took the teeth from the cod's mouth and forced them into his own. He made a few distorted faces then spat the teeth into his hand before throwing them into the sea with a cry of, 'They're not mine; they don't fit.'

Two toothless men, both now fed up, approached the Deal shore.

Albert said, 'Did you mark where you caught that big cod?'

Cuthbert said, 'Of coursh I did. I made a mark on the shide of the boat wiff me knife jusht where I got him.'

'I'm fishing with an idiot!' said Albert. 'Made a mark on the boat? Use your head. He'll probably give us a different boat nexsht time.'

Twenty-eight

A RATIONED
CHRISTMAS

I was born in 1948, which meant that for the first few years of my life there was still post-war rationing. The U-boat decimation of the trans-Atlantic convoys had ceased but only the essentials were being shipped. Petrol, clothing, furniture and food were only available through Ration Books; so much per person. Oddly, tobacco and alcohol always seemed available. as a small boy I had no need of tobacco or petrol, but I did hear of something that we couldn't get that I would like – Christmas pudding. Luxuries like spices, exotic fruits and cane sugar only became available in the shops in the mid-1950s. Christmas pudding was something you only read about in storybooks. It sounded wonderful.

One autumn morning in 1952 the postman knocked at my Grandparents' front door and handed my Grandfather a heavy parcel tied with string and sealing wax and labelled 'Perishable', 'By Sea' and 'Via Suez'. Gramps realised that it was from our relatives out in Australia and being a careful man he started to unpick the many knots in the string, his tongue pushing his bottom lip out making him look like a monkey. He never cut a piece of string in his life, saving all the pieces carefully in an old toffee tin. My Grandmother wasn't quite so patient; she snatched the parcel

from his hands, took it to the kitchen table and cut the string with the carving knife. Off came the brown paper revealing an old metal ammunition box, the lid sealed on with yet more gummed tape. Soon the lid was off.

The top item was a fat grey envelope. My granny opened it carefully discovering a fair quantity of dust-coloured granular fragments. She sniffed it but it smelled of nothing. She put it to one side and opened the next package.

Heavy waxed paper wrapped around sticky compressed dates. The next envelope contained ground cinnamon. Granny smiled as the smell filled the kitchen. Then a bag of sultanas, another of raisins and then some candied orange and lemon peel in waxed paper. There was a flat tin containing flaked almonds and a whole nutmeg, with the lacy mace still on it. Two lemons. Mixed spice in a paper bag. More waxed paper containing sticky dark cane sugar. A bag of currants. Granny chuckled to herself. It would only need some flour, a few breadcrumbs, a couple of eggs and some suet and here were all the ingredients for a Christmas pudding. As for the brandy, well, that would be found somewhere.

She took the large glazed crazed mixing bowl down from the shelf and tipped in all the ingredients. Suet and eggs from the larder, flour from the bin and breadcrumbs from an old Kilner jar were added to the bowl. A quick rootle through the bottom of the hall cupboard revealed a 'celebrations only' bottle from before the war. A few good glugs of brandy were poured in. My older cousin Janice turned up and joined in having a 'stir and a wish' of the wonderful mixture. That was when the lucky silver three-penny pieces were scattered into the sticky stuff. Then my Nan wrapped it all up in a cloth and put it over the 'copper' in the corner of the kitchen to steam.

Janice whispered in my ear. 'Let's get drunk,' she said, 'that steam is all alcohol 'cos all the brandy boils off first. We can lick it off the French windows when they steam up.' Janice was eighteen months older than me and very clever.

Maybe we did get drunk, or perhaps we just thought we did, but the pudding was cooked and placed in the larder until Christmas day when it would be steamed again. But one week before Christmas the letter arrived that should have accompanied the food parcel. It read something like this:

Dear Bob and Grace,

Hello from all in Toowoomba. We're about ninety miles from Brisbane and believe it or not you pass through a place called 'Ipswich' to get there, what a laugh! We will all be thinking of you in your wintery cold this Xmas; we will be on the sunny beach for a barby on Xmas day as this is the middle of our summer. It will be a big gang of us. There will be Roger and me, Suzy and husband Kerr and her new baby Ken and Roger's boss Frank and his wife and our neighbours the Robertsons with their two kids.

My brother (your second cousin) Paul won't be there though.

I'm sorry to say that he came down with a bug last winter so he was
sent to hospital and he passed away in his sleep. In his will he asked
that his ashes (top envelope in the food parcel) be scattered from
Westminster Bridge in London where our Dad was a lighterman
for so many years. Could you do that for me and say a few words?

Wishing you all the best and a happy Xmas.

Lots of love,

Mary XXX

Where were Uncle Paul's ashes now? They were in the Christmas
pudding. My Nan died peacefully in the 1970s but I never did find
out whether she took a sticky, half-cooked Christmas pudding all
the way to London on the train and lobbed gooey lumps of it into
the Thames while saying 'ashes to ashes' et cetera or whether she
kept quiet about the whole affair. In which case we all ate him with
brandy butter and very tasty he was too.

Twenty-nine

THE SWEEPER'S TALE

Many years ago a strangely twisted old man could be seen every day vigilantly sweeping the streets around Mews Gate at Charing Cross in central London. He was a curious figure; his clothes were no more than rags hanging over his crooked back, his hair was sparse under a rough cap and his eyes deep-set with the long view that sailors will develop after years on the oceans. His body was wiry and strong although his neck was habitually bent forward and to the right. His manner was cautious; his eyes darted up and down the street as if he were being hunted. His speech was slurred and rasping so that few would stop to listen to his ravings of 'innocence' long enough to discover what he may have ever done to be innocent of. One day he was simply not there; when the needs of heavier, wider traffic caused the demolition of the Mews Gate he disappeared with it; eventually a man was hired to sweep the streets of the accumulated rubbish. This is the old bent Sweeper's Tale.

It seems that some 300 years ago there was a young Canterbury man by the name of Ambrose Gwinett. He was twenty-two years old, in vigorous good health and articled to an attorney. He decided one day, in the winter of 1709, to visit his married sister. She and her husband kept an inn in the village of Ringwould, some three miles out of the Kentish coastal town of Deal. Being a healthy young man he cheerfully resolved to walk the eighteen miles along the country paths and roads to the coast. It was this very walk that decided the outcome of the remainder of his interesting life.

When he set off it was a bitterly cold winter's day with a strong sleet-filled easterly wind. He took the country paths to Bekesbourne and trudged through the bare groves of fruit trees to Adisham. On he went through the tiny hamlets of Chillenden, Tilmanstone and Betteshanger. At Northbourne he rested in a fine church porch and tried to remember how much further he had to go this foul day.

Despite his thick coat the wild weather wore him out; the cold wind scoured his face and when he eventually reached Mongeham and Deal his coat was so sodden and heavy that he felt that he could not walk no further. The prospect of an extra three miles up the long Dover road out of Walmer, across the exposed Hawksdown and Thistledown to Ringwould was too much, even for this young man. He decided to stay the night in a local pub. But it was now late in the day and fleets of ships were in Sandwich Haven and the Downs, sheltering from the storm; the town was full of sailors on shore leave. The Marine barracks were overflowing so inns were full as were hotels and guest houses. The only room offered to him was in a beachside alehouse, The Mermaid, and this was to be shared with a Mr Collins.

'Now, note that the door latch string is broken,' explained Mr Collins when they were introduced to each other, 'you will need to borrow my penknife to poke through the hole and lift the latch if you need to go out during the night.' He indicated a knife on the bedside chair. Mr Collins was large with a fruity voice, a nose red with broken veins and a bandage on his arm.

During the night Ambrose felt around to borrow the knife and left the room in the dark to go to the toilet in the yard. He politely did not light the lamp or a candle for fear of waking the snoring Mr Collins. When he opened the pocket-knife a gold guinea fell out, so he pocketed it to return it later. He did not disturb Mr Collins on his return.

Before dawn the next morning Ambrose rose in the wintery dark, found his coat drying by the embers of the huge fire downstairs and walked down Walmer Strand and along the Dover road to Ringwould to see his sister. She, with his brother-in-law, ran The Five Bells, the popular public house on Front Street.

She was mopping the public bar floor as he came in but she immediately dropped the mop, greeted him with some warmth and had soon prepared him a hearty breakfast. However, no sooner had he sat down and taken the first mouthful that there came a fierce hammering on the inn door.

Four burly policemen marched in, shackled Ambrose, picked him up by the elbows then marched him outside to throw him into their Police Cart. The brother-in-law ran out to them and asked the officials what had happened and why they were taking Ambrose away.

'Dire business in Deal town; not that it's any of your business, sir. This fellow slept in a shared room last night and his companion has disappeared, leaving nothing but a blood-soaked bed sheet and a trail of gore in the yard outside.' His face set in anger. 'And now, look, as we search Mr Gwinnet's pockets what do we find? Here is a clasp-knife; just as the landlord described to us as belonging to poor Mr Collins.'

He held out the stolen article for the brother-in-law to see. 'You'll have to follow us to Deal, maybe to Maidstone, if you want to see him at trial.' Ambrose's sister ran out of the inn holding the coat for her shirt-clad brother but the wagon rolled away into the freezing fog.

He was taken to Deal where a magistrate curtly committed him to the assizes in the County Court in Maidstone. He was taken there, still in his shirt, in an open cart through that bitter weather and tried for murder. Once there he was quickly found guilty, although there was little evidence to convict him. He was again taken in the open cart all the way back to Deal where he was hanged by the neck on a temporary gallows outside the very inn on the beach where Mr Collins had disappeared. A fearful gale stormed in from the East soaking and chilling the

officers, the priest and the hangman so that the execution was a
very hasty affair.

As quickly as possible the body was lowered and taken to
Ringwould. There it was suspended in irons and hung in a gibbet
on The Butts, a grassy field where the local men used to have their
weekly archery practice, not far from his sister's pub. That evening
a boy walking a herd of cows home past the gibbet looked up at the
body – it always gave him a thrill to see a dead criminal in irons –
but this time the corpse opened its eyes, blinked and looked back
at him. The man was still alive.

The cold weather had part-frozen him in the wagon from
Maidstone, this had prevented his neck breaking and he had been
cut down before he could be choked to death. The boy gave a
strangled gasp and ran into the pub with the shocking news that

the supposedly dead corpse was staring and blinking. Ambrose's sister and her husband took him down and looked after him, wondering if he would be tried and hung again.

He, too, was worried that he would be retried and again found guilty and sentenced to death for a second time. He was so concerned that he was taken the next day under a canvas in the pub cart across the Romney Marsh to Rye where he paid to be enlisted on a French privateer, a kind of legalised pirate ship. He made a strange sight; his neck was crooked, his face was swollen and the clothes he had borrowed from his brother-in-law were several sizes too big. His voice was but a croak from the bruising of the hangman's rope. His intention was to be beyond the reach of British Law, to travel across the Continent and find his fortune. However, the privateer was attacked off the French coast by a Spanish cruiser, an independent warship, and he was captured and ended up in a Havana jail in the Caribbean.

For three years he languished there but one day, as he was walking round the prison yard for his daily exercise, he was struck by the familiarity of the face of another prisoner. That red nose and that face; surely that was Mr Collins, the very man he had been hanged for murdering. He was thinner than Ambrose remembered but all the prisoners were thin; prison food was scarce and of very poor quality unless you had the money to buy better. Was Mr Collins real, or was he an apparition? Ambrose called out softly in a croak. 'Mr Collins?'

The man turned round and glared at Ambrose. 'Who wants to know?' was his terse response. Ambrose was cautious and spoke slowly, his damaged throat blurring his words, 'Have you ever been to England; specifically Deal in Kent, sir? It's a small seaside town north of Dover.'

'Deal? The last time that I trod on good British soil was in that very town, Deal it was, sir. It was one of the many places in which I sold my apothecary wares. Bensons Unguents, Ointments and Potions were my trade, sir, from Devon to Kent all along the south coast. What do you know of the place and why do you ask of it?'

Ambrose took a deep breath. 'Well, sir, I believe that we have met before, several years ago. I am sure that you are the very person with whom I shared a room one cold winter's night at the Mermaid Inn on Deal sea-front. You lent me your knife to lift the latch of the door. Do you remember?'

'Remember? Of course I remember. That was the very last day of my life as a travelling salesman. It was that very night that a clumsy barber sealed my fate.'

'And what was that fate? I must ask — I must know — for what happened to you had a profound effect upon my own life.'

Mr Collins slumped down and rested his back against the prison wall. 'I have rehearsed that night in my mind during long watches aboard ships and in cold nights in prison cells. I try to think of anything that I could have done to prevent my fate. At the time I only had business in three more Kentish chemists; in Eastry, Sandwich and Ramsgate and I had sold out of most things — the end of my route, you see. I had thought that day of making my way back to my home in Plymouth but there was a terrible storm and I decided to travel the next day. Oh, if only I had. But I had a terrible ache in my limbs and my head swam. A little too much port I expect. That is why I visited the barbers to be bled that day.'

'That was the bandage upon your arm, was it?'

Mr Collins' nodded and continued:

That was indeed staunching the wound where the blood-letting had been done. But the barber was a fool who used a new-fangled mechanical scarificator to pierce the skin. What a mess he made. By the time you arrived the wound had opened again. I had hoped that it would heal as I slept. But during the night my arm felt wet with blood and there was no sign of you around to help me bind it. I could not manage to tie the knots with one hand so I went out to visit the barber again. No matter what the hour, he must put right his poor work, I felt.

Ambrose listened, thinking of that fateful night, before saying:

Quite right and proper, too. But why, oh why did you not return to the Mermaid? Your disappearance was the very cause of this bent neck and my present imprisonment. I was accused, tried and hanged for your murder. Did you continue your sales trip? Where on Earth did you go?

Mr Collins, took in the crooked-necked man's story before going on with his own:

It was like this. The barber was a surly character and took some persuading to open his door after midnight but eventually he had re-bandaged my arm and I was back into that wild stormy weather with but a few paces to bring me to the Mermaid. I was just crossing the street to the alehouse when I was lifted from my feet by several men, carried across the shingle beach and thrown into a boat. My head hit something and when I came to my senses I was aboard a French privateer moored off the South Downs. The captain was a rough, surly Dutch cove who couldn't keep a crew and was annoyed that his remaining men had seized a fat injured man to replace them. He was all for throwing me overboard until he discovered my knowledge of medicine.

'A privateer, hey? That was how my adventures started, but I sailed from Rye and willingly,' Ambrose interjected; as Mr Collins concluded his story:

The Dutchman, for all his poor manners, was a mass of ailments, some real enough but others imaginary. As the storm blew over the next morning we set sail for the Mediterranean. Two days later off Finisterre we were attacked by a Portuguese privateer. I was captured and made physician to that crew and the captain of that ship. When the Spanish captured that ship I was put ashore and imprisoned here as you see me now.

They talked until they were locked into their cells. Over the next weeks they would meet every exercise time and plan their escape.

They were, by then, deeply tanned and Mr Collins had picked up enough of the Spanish language to pass as a Caribbean Spaniard. Ambrose would play the part of an idiot mute and together they planned an escape.

They did manage to trick their way out of prison and away from Havana, although through bad luck and worse weather they were again separated before they regained English soil; Ambrose was again imprisoned, this time in Algeria, and Mr Collins once again simply disappeared.

So now you know why the sweeper was bent and poorly spoken. You can appreciate why his attention was drawn to the appearance of any uniform on the street. But you don't know where he went when the Gate was pulled down – and nor do I.

Thirty

THE VANISHING
TRACTOR

I was visiting a small school for the day in Chilham, a tiny village a few miles south-east of Canterbury, to share some storytelling with the pupils and staff. At nine o'clock I walked into the reception area and could smell the pungent aroma of cooking cabbage.

Now nobody likes over-cooked greens, least of all me. If this was intended for the school lunch it would be cooking for three hours; about two and three-quarter hours too long. Despite my usual habit of eating with the students I decided that I would explore the nearby pub for my mid-day meal. The morning went well and later I found myself in The Woolpack, an oak-beamed fifteenth-century establishment which boasted a crackling log fire in an enormous inglenook fireplace and also (reputedly) a friendly 'Grey Lady' ghost.

The only other customers were a couple of men who enquired what I was doing in Chilham with a feather in my hat. I explained that I am a storyteller and what I did in schools and at other places and they showed polite interest. I asked what they were doing there and asked if they were local and if they had heard the story of the 'Grey Lady'.

'No,' they said, 'we're not local anywhere. We're travellers, properly known as Roma. You'd probably call us 'Gypsies' but it isn't right.

We're staying down the road towards Ashford and we don't know nothing about no Grey Lady.'

'Then you must know some of the old Roma stories,' I said in some excitement, 'you would have heard them told to you. Do you remember any?'

I should explain that we storytellers are very keen on hearing stories rather than reading them, especially if they come from a genuine source. A Welsh story from a Welsh person, a Roma story from a real traveller and so on. However, I was soon disappointed.

'Nagh, we don't do stuff like that no more. We got the telly; an' videos. Sittin' round the campfire of an evenin' listenin' to stories went out when me dad was young. Now his dad was a teller, and no mistake.'

'Did you ever hear any stories from your Grandfather, then?' I persisted.

'Can't remember any if he did,' said the traveller shortly, and we let the conversation drop.

I was just saying goodbye to the landlord and the travellers when one of them said, 'Of course, you wouldn't be interested in a story about a disappearin' tractor, would you?'

At last. Yes, of course I was interested. The school could wait a few minutes. I bought drinks for them both and sat down again with the two men. The one with the big moustache took a deep swig of beer, wiped his mouth and started the tale.

> Well, we always move on with the seasons and go where the work is. We was here in 1960s when me dad was a lad; and before that in the 1940s his dad had a place down in the King's Woods south of here. One day, when I were a lad in the 1960s, dad and me were walking up in Perry Woods after a couple of rabbits or a pigeon but me dad hadn't brought a gun. Then me dad told me what we were really there for.

He took a deep draught of his beer and cleared the foam off his moustache.

> Back in the 1940s, he said, me Grandfather had walked with him in those woods just as we were walking that day. The difference was that back then they had a horse with them. A big strong cob he were and he were towing a tractor. Me granddad told me dad that someone had 'given it him' and that he couldn't get any diesel to run it, what with wartime rationing an' all, but that he would put it somewhere safe until he found someone to buy it off him. It weren't that new; it were a Ferguson-Brown but it were in good nick and greased up and somebody would buy it. They found one of those flinty hollows, know what I mean? All through the Perry Woods there's these here pits, I think people have dug 'em for the chalk. He said he and my Grandfather had picked a good deep pit and got the horse to pull the tractor in. Then they covered it up.

All the time he had been talking he had been rolling a thin cigarette. Now he lit up.

> Me dad said that he knew exactly where the pit was; exactly halfway between The Pulpit and the pub. The Pulpit is the viewing spot, you seen it? The pub's the 'Rose and Crown'. Anyway, we found the place no trouble at all. There was the pit, all right, now with a great elm growing out of it; we poked about an' dug a bit but no flaming tractor. Me dad cursed and blinded and said someone must have nicked it and

you couldn't trust no one these days
so after searching around for
an hour or so we gave up and
we went off home. Me dad
still went on and on as we
walked back, grumpy you
see? When I picked up a few
nuts and stuck them in me
pocket he swore at me and
said 'That's just like your old

Grandfather; always pickin' stuff up. Pockets full
of rubbish. And head full of rubbish,too. He were
forgetful. He left his jacket under the tractor that
day, never saw it again.

The Roma took a deep drag on his fag.

Anyway, I dwelt on this when we got home and when I were in
bed I had a thought. I've always been a bit of a thinker, me. In the
morning I said to dad, 'I think I know where that ol' tractor is'. He
said 'No you bloody don't,' but he still came with me up to Perry
Woods later that day.

I lead him back to the pit and when we got there he said 'Well?'
and I pointed into the elm branches up above. And you know what?
Perched up there like a great bird up in the branches was the tractor.
Me grandpa had left elm seeds, you know, the ones with wings, in
his pocket and left his jacket under the tractor. One of them had
taken and lo! A tree had grown.

The Roma looked me square in the eyes as if challenging me to call
him a liar.

'And it went for £300. Collector's piece, you see. Now you had
better go and tell some of your old todge to those kids. I haven't
got any more lies to tell you.'

Thirty-one

THE WISE OLD FOOL

Sitting comfortably astride a milestone on one of the roads into Sandwich was the town fool. He was seen there in all weathers; snow encrusted his feathered hat in the cruel winters, the Kentish sun broiled him as it ripened the fruit in the orchards and the corn in the fields.

One cool spring morning a horse and rider approached from the north. As they came level with the milestone and the old man they stopped. The well-dressed rider leaned over and bellowed to the fool, 'I say, my man, are you a resident of this town?' His eyes scanned the roofs and church towers down the road. 'I am thinking of moving to a bigger, better place.'

The old man fixed the rider with a steady gaze from under the brim of his battered hat.

'Sir, I have lived here in Sandwich, on and off, for over sixty years.'

'That will do. Now tell me, what are the people like hereabouts?'

'Well, sir, that depends.'

'Can you not give me a direct answer, you old fool? Depends? Depends upon what?'

'It depends on what you mean by "people" and what you mean by "like". For instance, what are the people like where you come from?'

'Ah, well, that is a very different matter. There I am something big in the town, a town councillor no less and for two years the

mayor of Ramsgate. And I am one of the
biggest, most successful businessmen in
the area. But the people there, they are
stand-offish. The neighbours never
speak except to complain, the shop-
keepers are surly and mean and the
children are noisy little thieves
and rascals. I swear that the
tailor, the butcher and the
baker raise their prices the
moment that I walk into their
shops. Besides which they all
gossip about my private life and
my business behind my back.
I will be glad to leave the
place, to be frank.'

'Well God bless you
sir, you will find here
that they are just the same. Mean,
cold, unfriendly and dishonest. No doubt about it.'

The man snorted in derision and spurred his horse to ride west
towards Canterbury. The old fool watched him disappear up the
Ash road with a wry smile on his worn face.

The seasons turn and the sun shines down generously. Easter has
come and gone and the leaves are the greenest they will ever be.
As the old fool still sits on the milestone and invents riddles in his
head there is the sound of a donkey approaching from the north.
Looking up the old man can see the figure of a woman gently
leading the beast and can half-hear her encouraging words that she
whispers into its ancient ear.

'Not far now, me lovely, one more mile and you shall have a
drink, a bite of turnip and a rest on some comfy straw.'

The fool spoke. 'Good day to you, my lady. A fine morning, is it
not?' A pair of friendly eyes fixed her in their hazel gaze.

A bright pair of blue eyes smiled back. 'A good morning to you,
sir. You seem to have an easy occupation, sitting out here in the sun.'

'You may think so, it may seem so, but this is a job that requires some subtlety. Twelve years ago there was a competition held to find the 'King of the Fools' for my town of Sandwich there down the road. I believe that I remember that for some reason all the other contestants withdrew, leaving me to take the title and be crowned with a coronet of knives, forks and spoons. There was a small sum of money attached to the post, too. So this old stone is my royal throne; I fulfil many of my foolish duties from here. And what brings you this way, my dear?'

'Oh, it is a sad business. I live just outside Ramsgate, have done all me married life. But now me husband has crippled his legs on one of them new reaper machines so the farmer has gone and sacked him and he's demanded that we leave our old cottage that we've been in for nigh on thirty years. It goes with the job, see? "A farm cottage for farm workers" he says. There is nowhere else to be had that we can afford in Ramsgate. So I'm scouting about for a new place to live. What's Sandwich like, then?'

'I am sorry to hear your sad news. Before I describe Sandwich to you, tell me, what was it like living in Ramsgate?'

'Well, I moved to St Lawrence in Ramsgate when I married Frank nearly forty years ago. I grew up in Northwood and I met Frank at a harvest supper when I was a slip of a girl. Northwood was nice 'cos you knew everyone but when we married Ramsgate turned out to be just the same. It was like being in a huge family; you could always find someone to lend you a spoonful of salt or to look after one of the kids for an hour. If you needed something there was always somebody who could get it, come the fruit ripening there was always baskets of cherries being swapped for a jar of honey or a leg of pork. Need help with a leaking roof and the whole village would be up there patching the holes. And laugh? I don't think there was a day went by when we didn't have a good belly laugh with somebody, even in the worst of times. No, I wouldn't leave if I didn't have to.'

The old fool looked at her and grinned widely. 'Here is the good news; the people are just the same in Sandwich; friendly, honest and kind. Do come to live here and I will guarantee that you will settle in just as if you were born here. You will be hugely welcome.'

Year after year the old fool sat and advised whether folk should move to Sandwich or not. He rarely gave the same advice twice; those who moved to Sandwich found that his prediction came true and they had happy lives. Those who he put off saying that the people were just the same in Sandwich as where they had come from found that his words were true in their case too. Perhaps a happy life is portable; you take it with you wherever you go.

NOTES

The Mirror – This is really only half-Kentish. The original first half was given by an ancient Indian teacher in Goa; I had asked at the hotel who knew the oldest stories and the reply was, 'Find the oldest female teacher in a school and she will have learned tales from her extended group of female relatives.' The oldest teacher turned out to be over ninety years old and beautifully spoken, educated in Cambridge in the 1930s. She told this tale up until the point where the wife saw the mirror but couldn't remember any more than that, 'I expect she forgave him in the end for I remember that she made him coffee,' she said.

Three years later I told the first half to the 'Dover Museum Trustees' Christmas Dinner and Dance' and at the end of the evening an old man came up to me and claimed that he knew the end of the story. I was surprised but he said that when he was a tiny boy he was taken for walks by his old great uncle who had been an importer/exporter for the East India Company. If he ever came across a piece of broken mirror his uncle would gaze into it and then cry 'Ghah, ugly old hag, throw it away!' The speaker puzzled over this especially when he discovered that 'hag' was a term for an ugly old female. He had wondered about it over the years until that very evening when he had surmised the end of the tale.

King Herla – The story of a hero visiting an unearthly land for much longer than he expected is common in Irish, Breton and Welch Celtic tales as well as in a charming Japanese version.

The Celtic Hero – Nothing much is known of Celtic humour although the Romans seem to have been the butt of jokes from many directions. For instance, a Roman noble was riding through the recently conquered Grecian countryside one morning when he was astonished to see his double; a man who shared all his features although he was obviously a slave. 'Was your mother ever in Rome about twenty years ago?' the noble jocularly enquired. 'No,' replied the slave, 'but my father was.'

Princess Rushycoat – There are parallels here with Cinderella and Shakespeare's King Lear, although in some earlier versions the daughter runs away because the king wants her to take the place of her dead mother at his side – and in his bed.

Death is Strongest – Another 'world tale' with relatives in Germany, Arabia, Italy and beyond. This turns up in Chaucer's *The Canterbury Tales* as 'The Pardoners Tale'. Together with 'Generous', also known as 'The Franklin's Tale', these were 'borrowed' by Chaucer from Italy or from tellers in Islamic Spain who themselves, I expect, found them originally as Hindu tales.

What Can You See? – This is one of the many variations of Chaucer's 'The Merchant's Tale'. The ending I stole from the delicatessen scene in the 1989 film *When Harry Met Sally*.

Grey Dolphin – I found this version in an online parish magazine written by Bill Hutchins (*St Georges' News*, 2003). The details vary from source to source but unquestionably there is a tomb to Robert Shurland, complete with carved horse head, in the Minster Abbey on the Isle of Sheppey.

Generous – See 'Death is Strongest'.

The Battle of Sandwich – A wonderful tale which mixes real historical events, characters and places with legend; I'm sure the French have a variation of this to tell.

The Hand of Glory – Another confection concocted for 'Ghost Walks' around Canterbury in the 1990s.

Pulling Game – This exists in England, Italy, Portugal and South America. I found it first in, of all places, *Readers Digest*.

Nell Cook and the Dark Passage – I adopted this from The Ingoldsby Legends for use in giving a Canterbury Ghost Tour.

The Three Feathers – This was collected from some Deptford Roma hop-pickers working on the Kentish harvest in the 1930s. There are many world tales of the unfortunate younger brother and how he succeeds. The Princess and the Fool is another. It has parallels in the Roma tales from Eastern Europe. In 'Mighty Jepas', for instance, the younger brother starts as a deformed cripple, handsome on the right side but warped on the left, but he wins the Princess despite this.

The Wantsum Wyrm – Many years ago an elderly and respected storyteller told this story to a meeting of other storytellers with the suggestion that it should be adapted to a variety of localities and retold wherever possible. This world tale was originally an Indian puzzle story called 'The Five Helpers' and it holds metaphysical meanings, the most obvious of which is the value of cooperation. I developed this for a meeting of organisations co-operating to preserve the Thanet coast.

That's Enough to be Going on With – I don't tell this tale as often as I could as it sounds a bit like a Victorian morality story promoting politeness.

Red Jacket – Also known as 'The Nose Tree', I heard this tale from a traveller during a Rural Activity Day just outside Ashford in the 1980s.

The Biter Bit – A little poetic justice here.

The Two Pickpockets – From Katherine Briggs' *Dictionary of British Folk-tales*. Ms Briggs had close associations with Kent and it was a lady just down the road in Sandwich who was given the task, after Ms Briggs' death, to deal with the fortune offered for the stories by a Japanese animation studio. By the way, warning notices like the one in this story are still used by pickpockets all over the world. I last saw one next to a cash machine in Covent Garden.

The Man Who Could Understand Animals – This tale, but with the husband beating his wife at the end, is the first to be told in the *1001 Arabian Nights* and is told to Scheherazade by her sister as an example of how to survive the King's bloody habits. It became Kentish when it was attributed to Shepherdswell by me many years ago.

Apple Tree Man – This, with the story 'That's Enough to be Going on With', was collected at a splendid place, Perry Court Farm, on the Canterbury road out of Ashford, where they were holding an autumn display of apples and pumpkins. They also had the great idea of hiring a storyteller.

Brave Mary of Mill Hill – Another universal tale; sometimes she is a blacksmith's daughter, in other versions the child of a gambling fisherman.

Grey Lady Woods – Part urban myths, part local gossip, the tales from this place were confirmed by the Deal Social Club for the Blind. In the past many blind people became musicians and storytellers.

A Kingsdown Romance – A world story that has been claimed as Japanese, Irish, Portuguese and more. I found it in the splendid book *Shapers and Polishers* by Betty Rosen. This was the tale that I told to a class of eight-year olds in Dover, with the intention that they should get into groups and work out how to retell the story each from a different perspective. The teacher took me to one side before I started and explained that one girl would be taking no notice of me at all and would not be creating with the others.

'She's not being rude, she has autism; it's as if all around her is nothing but a dream. But she always wants to come to school, although she has never stood up or spoken here in four years of attendance.' The groups retold the story as a mini opera, as an MTV news bulletin, as a committee meeting of the local 'Women's Institute' and lastly from the point of view of the mermaid's family. This last group included the autistic girl who, during the retelling, stood up and made strange gestures in the air. The teacher had never seen her stand before and rushed forward.

'What are you doing, dear?' the teacher asked.

'Hanging up starfish to dry of course,' was the halting reply.

She had entered the story; somehow this old tale had penetrated her mental isolation. I felt like a gorilla who had found a surgeon's tool bag; wonderful glittery things but how are they supposed to be used? Stories have been used as healing tools in some societies and here was I using them as mere diversions.

The Seaside and the Londoners: Proper Fishing – An early urban myth, as is 'The Seaside and the Londoners: Lil'. These started to become well known with the advent of the railway services to the coast.

A Rationed Christmas – I have no idea where this urban myth came from but apparently there were versions of it circulating back before the Napoleonic wars. It should, of course, be told at the Christmas dinner table, timed so that the first mouthful of pudding coincides with the last line. Your own fictitious family details should be used for maximum affect if told as true.

The Sweeper's Tale – Thanks first of all to Mr Friend of the Deal Social Club for the Blind. It was he who lent me a copy of this story and started a long search in which I discovered pages from an old 1930s copy of the *East Kent Mercury* giving the lyrics of a song; an association to a Victorian performance at a theatre in Hull and possibly Daniel Defoe using a pseudonym. Weirdly an internet search for the name 'Ambrose Gwinnet' revealed these to be the two first names of Ambrose Bierce, the fantasy writer.

The Vanishing Tractor – Much as I heard it from the gentlemen in the Chilham pub as described.

The Wise Old Fool – This useful tale has been in my head it seems forever. Since 2008 I have been 'King of the Fools' in Sandwich, a position gained in much the same way as in the story, although in my case I was dragged backwards through the town while three street bands played three different tunes at once. I was then ennobled with the crown of knives, forks and spoons. My fool's office is outside in 'No Name Street' which, now that it sports a metal street sign advertising this name, is a celebrated paradox.

BIBLIOGRAPHY

BOOKS:

Allhusen, E., *Fopdoodle & Salmagundi* (Old House Books, 2007)

Bignell, A., *Kent Lore* (Robert Hale, 1983)

Briggs, K., *Dictionary of British Folk-tales* (Routledge, 1971)

Clouston, W.A., *Clouston Book of Noodles* (Gale Research, 1969)

Doel, F & G., *Folklore of Kent* (Tempus Publishing, 2003)

Frost, T., *In Kent with Charles Dickens* (Tinsley Bros, 1880)

Hillier, C., *The Bulwark Shore* (Eyre Methuen, 1980)

Johnson, W.H., *Kent Stories of the Supernatural* (Countryside Books, 2000)

Major, A., *Kentish As She Wus Spoke* (S.B. Publications, 2001)

Nye, R., *Classic Folk Tales of the World* (Bracken Books, 1994)

Saunders, H.W., *The History of Kent* (John Murray, 1936)

Setford, L., *Kent Folklore & Legends* (James Pike Ltd, 1977)

Shah, I., *World Tales* (Allan Lane, 1979)

OTHER SOURCES:

Hutchins, B., *St Georges' News*, (Online Parish Magazine, 2003)

Reader's Digest, *Folklore and Legends of Britain* (1977)